ONE KNIGHT'S
Journey

Perspective of a
Knights of Columbus
State Deputy

SCOTT A. O'CONNOR

lectio

Lectio Publishing, LLC
Hobe Sound, Florida, USA

www.lectiopublishing.com

Photos in this book are owned by the author or used with permission.
Harry Rother, Florida State Photographer: pages 47, 73–98.
Randy Hale, Former State Photographer: inside front cover; page 54; inside rear cover (Saltillo).
O'Connor Family Archives: Chapter 1.
All other photos, property of the Author.

Cover and Book Design: Linda A. Wolf

Paperback ISBN 978-1-943901-29-6
Library of Congress Control Number: 2022950392

November 2022.
2d printing, December 2022.

Published by Lectio Publishing, LLC
Hobe Sound, Florida 33455
www.lectiopublishing.com

Front cover: Installation as a Supreme Director, Basilica of Our Lady of Guadalupe, Dallas Tex., October 2021. L to R: Supreme Chaplain Most Reverend William E. Lori, Archbishop of Baltimore; Scott A. O'Connor; Supreme Knight Patrick E. Kelly; Mrs. Vanessa Kelly.
Inside cover: State Chaplain Msgr. Thomas J. Skindeleski with first-class relic of St. John Paul II.

2-2-2023

To Sean Williams,

thank you for the amazing work you are doing with our Agents, and for always letting me bounce ideas off you. It really means a lot to me.

Fraternally

[signature]

DEDICATION

To the memory of John Leonard, the first man to invite me to join the Knights of Columbus. John was a faithful Catholic and a dedicated Knight of Columbus, also, William Braun, Jr., the man responsible for getting me to my First Degree and supporting my advancement through the ranks. I also want to recognize my late wife, Marybeth O'Connor, for her dedication and support of our seminarians; vocations support was the cornerstone of our administration and her dedication and accomplishments were many.

CONTENTS

FOREWORD

If someone were to ask me, what was it that attracted me to that Catholic men's fraternity known as the
Knights of Columbus, and why I became a member, I
would readily offer to them to read Scott O'Connor's mini-
autobiography, *One Knight's Journey: a Perspective of a
Knights of Columbus State Deputy*. In doing so, I believe
that they would then understand why so many men came
to the same conclusion as I did to become a member. His is
a true to form and splendid explanation of what has drawn
more than two million men worldwide in their journey to
get to heaven in a world filled with very challenging hu-

man situations and complex issues.

The founder of the Knights of Columbus Order, Blessed Michael McGivney, had a wonderful insight into the problems that plagued our society during his time. He immediately set about doing what he humanly could do to alleviate the sufferings of the underprivileged. The problems he faced—not really different than the present-day ones we have, were usually brought about by the indifference of so many in leadership; so he used his God-given ability to organize Catholic men in a joint effort to deal with the situation. Each day he called upon God's help to search for the right means to fulfill that destiny.

Scott O'Connor tells us, in a very personal way, how he, too, has tried to use whatever means God gave him and to open his mind and heart to God's powerful yet gentle message in a world loaded with many distractions. His story, filled with a number of personal anecdotes and some unusual and quite interesting experiences, is the result of taking time during the Covid-19 pandemic to reflect upon how God works in our world: not so much through spectacular means, but in unique ways to guide us to our ultimate destiny. Since our responsibility is to live each day in a way that enables us to best use God's gifts for the good of others and ourselves, Scott takes the very human situations of life—complete with its ups and downs—and shows us his way of using those gifts and talents to achieve our Columbian goals.

It's been a great joy of mine as a State Chaplain to know and have worked with Scott for over a decade, watching him grow the Order and grow within the Order by using his Catholic faith, background, experience, and common sense to exemplify the pillars of our Order—charity, unity, fraternity and patriotism. When you read his story, you may find some common thread in your own life story that will help draw you closer to God through service and love for our neighbor. I highly recommend this book to you!

Monsignor Thomas J. Skindeleski
Florida K of C State Chaplain Emeritus

* * *

Jesus, help me to simplify my life by learning what You want me to be and becoming that person.

St. Therese of Lisieux offered this simple prayer to God containing the goal that all should strive to attain.

Scott A. O'Connor offers in this book a journey of life, death, and new life. It is the meaning of each Catholic Christian's pilgrimage on earth. Following Jesus Christ and His example, we who are believers understand that there is a life lived, a death experienced and a new life in eternity. All made possible through grace given by God alone.

This book offers lessons in servant-leadership modeled on the authentic leadership of Jesus Christ. Authenticity Jesus Christ taught his followers in the parable of the Good Shepherd. For followers to fully place their trust in a leader there must be three elements present: an intimate relationship with the leader; a recognition that following the leader will lead to the good of the follower; and the knowledge that the leader will sacrifice for his or her followers. This authentic love offered by the Good Shepherd has echoed through history in the life of the saints and martyrs to the very time of Blessed Michael J. McGivney in 1882 upon the foundation of the Knights of Columbus.

Those who knew Blessed Michael McGivney best in life saw in both a "genial countenance and a man with an indomitable will to achieve the good. In sum his founding of the Knights of Columbus attests to the love in which he held his fellow brother/man." In the spirit of the principles upon which each Knight of Columbus pledges to follow: Charity, Unity, Fraternity and Patriotism, the author is a living exemplification and clarion call to Columbianism. One Knight's Journey travels from life to death to new life. It is the pilgrimage of a loving good shepherd filled with God's grace. It offers the reader markings on the road of a life that begins and ends with God.

VIVAT JESUS! (MAY JESUS LIVE!)

Mark W. Lynn, PhD

ACKNOWLEDGEMENTS

There are so many people whom I would like to pay tribute to, for their support, encouragement, and friendship along my faith journey; however, that would take another book. But I do want to recognize the following individuals who significantly impacted my life, for the good:

I thank my late wife Marybeth (Stodolski) O'Connor who first awakened in me an awareness of the presence of the Holy Spirit and started me on my faith journey. To Marybeth, I shall always be grateful and shall cherish the memories of our 43 years together. I am grateful to my immediate family, Magen, David, Alexis, Lauren, Andrew, and Jeffrey, I am so proud of the amazing people you are and have become. To Monsignor William "Bill" McDonnell, who first administered the Sacraments to me, thank you for your long service to the Church and your friendship now into the fifth decade. To my pastor of many years at St. Bonaventure Catholic Church, Father Edmund Prendergast, you have been there for my children, you married my oldest daughter and baptized my first grandson, you were there for my mother's memorial and my late wife's funeral. You are a great inspiration as well as a great friend. To my brother and sister-in-law Barbara and Greg Byrne, thank you for your support, your prayers and your help. I thank my nephew Fr. Matthew Byrne, for your prayers and support.

I am especially grateful to the following individuals who took extensive time and effort to review and critique *One Knight's Journey:* Monsignor Thomas Skindeleski, State Chaplain Emeritus, who provided insight and improved the reading significantly. Monsignor Tom you are now and shall forever be part of the family, your friendship is priceless to me; and to Joe Cox, an amazing author and teacher in his own right and a true Brother Knight who helped wordsmith this manuscript into something much better than what I could do on my own; to Most Reverend Patrick C. Pinder, Archbishop of Nassau, Bahamas, for your most kind foreword and for being not only an amazing religious leader but for being such a good friend and advisor.

I would like to express my gratitude to all the amazing people that share my passion for the work that the Knights of Columbus provide. The following have played a significant role in my journey as a leader in the Knights of Columbus, beginning with the two men who first suggested that I become a Knight, John Leonard and Ray Farrell; and then William "Bill" Braun, PGK, PFN, who was the man responsible for me entering the Order and joining St. Bonaventure Council No. 12240 in Davie, Florida; to Robert "Bob" Dytkowski, who as District Deputy helped me achieve success as a Grand Knight; I thank Tommy Thompson, PGK, PFN, FDD, and Former District Marshal, for his mentoring and taking me under his wing, Tommy was the first to see in me the potential for leadership in the Order; to Robert "Bob" Read, PSD, FM, who gave me the opportunity to serve as a District Deputy and to further develop my leadership skills; to Gary McLain, PSD, FM, FVSM, who gave me the opportunity to join the 4th Degree Exemplar Team, an amazing group of dedicated men who truly believe in the principles of our Order; to Doug Murray, PSD, who gave me my first opportunity to serve at the State level, Doug saw in me the potential to advance our jurisdiction's capabilities, and we did just that. I also want to acknowledge other past state deputies, who each one of you contributed to whatever success I may have achieved, you are or were, all amazing people, dedicated to the principles of Charity, Unity, Fraternity and Patriotism: Donald Kahrer, Don Goolesby, Deacon Paul Koppie, Chris Kernan, Doug Murray, Jim Schoenfeld, Bob Read, Stan Zurzinski, Dave Tebo, Dennis Stoddard, John Hemel (D), Jerry Grillo (D), Gary McLain, Bob Anderson (D), Thomas Shaughnessy, Jim Cupp, Frank Scandone, and Dick LaLuzerne.

I am also grateful to many of the people with whom I have had the pleasure of working, who also serve in leadership positions: David Tebo, PSD, FM, Territorial Growth Director, who has been a friend, supporter, mentor and advisor; to Jose Jimenez, PSD, a Vice President of Hispanic Development and in charge of the southeast for membership growth. Jose, you have been a strong supporter and helped me immensely during the most difficult of times, you are a true Knight of the Order. To my friend Chris Lewis, President of The American Wheelchair Mission, thank you for our support and your friendship, going with you to Mexico on a wheelchair distribution project was truly an experience of a lifetime. To the Supreme Officers, Directors, and individuals at the headquarters of the Order, with whom I worked during my time as State Deputy; especially John Marrella, Supreme Advocate, and Dennis Stoddard, Supreme Master. Both offered wise counsel, guidance and support whenever I needed it. I thank our past Supreme Knight, Carl Anderson, for his support; I thank our current Supreme Knight, Patrick Kelly, for his support, his vision and his friendship.

There were many people who were with me as I started

my leadership journey, however, life happens, some have gone to their eternal rest, others may have moved out of the area and some just dropped off along the path, but there are several Knights who have supported me all along the journey, I want to especially thank them for being not only dedicated to the vision of Blessed Michael McGivney, but also committed to the goals that we set: Brother Ron Brown, PGK, PFN, FDD and State Ceremonials Director, thank you for your unwavering support and your friendship; Brother George Hayek, PGK, PFN, FDD, and former State Marketing and Brands Director, Brother George, you helped to move the jurisdiction into the modern world, I am so very proud of your accomplishments; Brother Mark Lynn, PGK, PFN, FDD and Past State Warden, Brother Mark, I thank you for all you have done for me and for keeping me focused on the Faith and what is truly important, you are my Brother from another Mother, but also you make me laugh, I think we share the same sense of humor. To Reverend Mr. Paul and Theresa Koppie, PSD, you two helped me through some of the darkest days, I could not have had the success we achieved if it was not for your involvement, I truly value your support and your friendship; to our current state board of directors: State Deputy Rob Urrutia and his wife Lucille, you are family, you have been great team members along the journey, I am proud to be witness to your continuing to build on the successes of the Florida Jurisdiction; to State Secretary Rick Hughes and his wife Melody, thank you for your service and your friendship; to Michael and Lisa Gizewski, our State Treasurer and his wife, you are amazing people who truly live the principle of Charity, every day, thanks for the memories; to Robert Rasch and his wife Peggy, our State Advocate, you were invaluable to me during my administration and you continue to provide expert advice. Your friendship means so much; to Joseph Coicou and his wife Shirley, our State Warden, you are the future, I have high hopes for your success, raising a large family in this time has its challenges but you are living examples of what "family" is supposed to be about, living the faith and serving as an example for your children. To Ed Sleyzak, State Marketing & PR Director; Harry Rother, State Photographer; Marc Andersen, State Merchandising Chairman; Scott Huetterman, Newsletter; John Medina, Communications; Joseph Purka, Jr., Public Relations, thank you for your service.

I want to mention several other clergy whom I have come to know and have benefited from our time together: Father Martin Dunne, III. Fr. Marty and I worked on degree teams together, long before he started the process of discerning to the priesthood, and before I had decided to run for state office in the Order. Fr. Sal Pignato, Former State Chaplain, Fr. Robert Kantor, State Chaplain, Fr. Chris Hoffmann, Florida District Friar. I also want to recognize the Florida Bishops whom I had the pleasure of working with: Most Reverend Thomas Wenski, D.D., Archbishop of Miami, Most Reverend Enrique Delgado, Auxiliary Bishop; Most Reverend Felipe Estevez D.D., Bishop 'Emeritus' Diocese of St. Augustine; Most Reverend Gregory Parkes, D.D., Bishop of St. Petersburg; Most Reverend John Noonan, D.D., Bishop of Orlando; Most Reverend William Wack, C.S.C., Bishop of Pensacola/Tallahassee; Most Reverend Gerald Barbarito, D.D., J.C.L., Bishop of Palm Beach; Most Reverend Frank Dewane, D.D., Bishop of Venice.

To the Florida General Agents: Jim Spinelli, FIC, CLU, LUTCF; Sergio Urrutia and Brian Lawandus, I am grateful for your counsel, your guidance, your support and your work efforts to make Florida a truly great jurisdiction, but most of all I thank you for your friendship.

I also want to give a shout out to my local council, St. Bonaventure, No. 12240 in Davie, Florida. So many men have come and gone, over the past two decades, but every one of them in some way had an impact on me.

To Father Frank Roof, who served as Council Chaplain for the better part of a decade, thank you for your service and your friendship, we have covered many miles together in faith. I shall always be grateful to you for your prayers and support for my late wife Marybeth; to Father Peter Sutinga, you are a beacon of light and a true 'good shepherd' of your flock, I love your enthusiasm for always looking to share the "good news." I am grateful for knowing Bill Braun, the founding Grand Knight, who gave me my start in the Order; to Denis Mello, the 2nd Grand Knight and person who pushed me to run for Grand Knight; Vincent

Manzo, a great Knight and Brother who is and always shall be one of my closest friends; Kevin Cary, who once told me "you are going to be the State Deputy someday" I did not think much of that at the time, but he was right; to Jude, Felix and James Hodges, you are like part of my family, we have been through so much together and I am grateful for your being part of my Faith Journey; to John Pisula, you continued to build upon the foundation of our council, thank you for your leadership and your enthusiasm; to Lawrence Franzoni, you are the present and will bridge the council into the future, thank you for your leadership; to Tom Finan, you stepped up and took on the Habitat for Humanity program at a time when we needed it the most, thanks for always being ready to serve; to my new friend Tim O'Connor (no relation) in a short time, you have made significant contributions to the Church, the Community and the Order. There are many more in the council who have impacted my life, to those of you I offer my sincere thanks.

I am grateful to Eric and Linda Wolf at Lectio Publishing, for taking a chance on this book and for all the help and support along the way, I value your input and your friendship.

Finally, as I enter a new chapter in my life, I am grateful to have known so many good people, many of whom have passed away, but I am also very grateful for the new friends that have come into my life, especially Joann, who has brought joy and laughter and puts a smile on my face, each time we are together on a new adventure.

CHAPTER 1

The Early Years

My great grandfather, Arthur Connolly, was probably the first member of my family to join the Knights of Columbus, sometime between 1910 and 1920. His daughter, my grandmother Helen (Connolly) O'Connor, on my father's side, whose parents had immigrated to the United States around the turn of the twentieth century, was the middle of five children, three boys and two girls. The oldest boy, Charles, only ten-years-old at the time, died from a drowning accident while trying to save his younger brother, John, who had fallen into a river. My great-grandmother (Mary McSorley) came directly from

Northern Ireland. She was from a large family, and it is rumored that she had several relatives who opened the McSorley's Ale House in the Bronx, New York. It has the distinction of being the oldest continuously operating brew house in the country.

Arthur Connolly was the patriarch of my father's family in the United States. Unfortunately, records do not go back far enough to locate his Knight's membership number. But I found references to his involvement in newspaper articles and in his obituary,

Top, L to R: Madeline Connolly, John Connolly, and Helen Connolly-O'Connor
Bottom L to R: Arthur Connolly, Francis Connolly, Mary McSorley-Connolly

which mentioned the Knights of Columbus. His parents had arrived in Canada from Ireland around the time of the great potato famine. Arthur immigrated to the USA from his birthplace in Canada.

He began his career as a blacksmith, but near the end of the nineteenth century new opportunities opened up in repairing automobiles, trucks, and other mechanized vehicles. Arthur settled in the central Iowa town of Waterloo where he opened his auto-body repair and paint shop. It was a family business. My grandmother, Helen, worked in the office, and my great uncles John and Frank worked in the shop with their father. Arthur was a pillar in his community, helping to build the Sacred Heart Catholic Church. He was active in parish life. The current Sacred Heart Catholic Church website (www.sacredheartwloo.org) states in its "Points in Our History" timeline that in January 1909, Archbishop John J. Keane granted the request to form a new parish in Waterloo. On March 4, 1909, Reverend J. J.

Hanley, then of Monti (Iowa), was appointed pastor. It then states that "3 trustees elected to assist in business affairs: J. L. Dunnwald, Arthur Connolly, and George McGuire." There is one more reference to my grandfather: "October 7, 1921: Father Molly and trustees Arthur Connolly and J. J. Meany replace old pew rent system with a new system, known as the envelope system. It was decided to give this a 1-year trial." That was the last entry that identified him.

Arthur Connolly was a patriot to his adopted country. He is seen in this photo taken on the very first Armistice Day, dressed as "Uncle Sam" riding in a parade. My Aunt Patricia "Pat" Minor told me that Grandfather Arthur was very much involved in his community and the Catholic Church. After Arthur's death, his obituary names the Knights of Columbus as participants in his funeral ceremony.

My grandmother, Helen, married Henry Roach O'Connor. He was born in the USA, though his parents had immigrated from Ireland earlier in the twentieth century. My father, Henry Arthur O'Connor, was the oldest of three children born to Helen and Henry Roach O'Connor. My father had a younger brother, James, the middle child, and a sister, Patricia. James was a Knight of Columbus. In his early years,

my father was an altar server and had been groomed to attend seminary. He spoke often about growing up on the Iowa plains, spending summers playing kick-the-can or stickball with neighborhood kids. But he was silent about growing up during the Great Depression, about his father leaving the family to find work elsewhere in the country.

My grandfather O'Connor was a banker. When the banks closed, he found himself in desperate times, making it hard for the family. Small pleasures meant a lot. My dad recounted how they followed the Ice-Man in the summer to get the ice chips that broke off—a real treat on a hot day. At the end of his high school years, my father's plans changed when the Japanese bombed Pearl Harbor and the USA entered World War II.

My father enlisted in the US Navy at seventeen. He had to have a permission slip signed by his mother to join, but in he went. He rarely talked about his time in the war. But one story came up. He drove an ambulance back to the Landing Ship Tank (LST) for transport of wounded to the hospital ships. On a particular day, he picked up a general in his ambulance, basically a jeep with a stretcher lashed to the back. My father was so nervous that he made

Henry O'Connor, my father.
World War II, Navy.

a turn too fast and flipped the jeep. He thought the general would see that he was court-martialed. To my father's surprise, the general dusted himself off, rounded up a couple of GIs and righted the jeep, got back in and said to my father, "Don't do that again," and off they went.

My father came home from the war and like many other G.I.s wanted to make up for lost time. He entered the University of Northern Iowa under the G.I. bill. There he met my mother, Erna Gravesen, the middle daughter of Christian Gravesen and Olga (Robenhagen). My mother looked up to her older sister, Gertrude, and usually emulated whatever Gertrude did. I learned that my Aunt Gertrude was one of the women pilots of the Women's Air Corp (WAC) who transported aircraft to the European theatre. My mother was too young to enlist but that did not stop her from learning to fly. In fact, she was half owner in a small Piper airplane. She told me how she once ran out of gas and had to ditch in a cornfield. The farmer came out to see what the fuss was all about, then pulled the airplane out of the field with his tractor!

My mother supported the war effort in many ways that included joining the Civil Air Patrol, where she served as the adjunct to the general. She worked in the family business, which consisted of a grocery store and filling station. She also helped with fundraising efforts to support the troops and managed to save enough money to enter college after the war.

My parents married right after their graduation from the University of Northern Iowa (UNI), where they received their undergraduate degrees; they immediately enrolled in graduate school at the University of Missouri, in Columbia. My father taught high school biology while working on his doctoral degree in education, completed in 1956. That same year he accepted a position at the then Northern Illinois State Teachers College—later to become Northern Illinois University—located in DeKalb, Illinois, about sixty miles west of Chicago. There I would be born in October of that same year.

My early memories of Knights of Columbus events include picking up fried fish, hushpuppies, and coleslaw at the K of C Hall. This was before fast-food drive throughs, and they would carry everything imaginable. While there may have been a few drive-through burger stores, only the Knights had drive-through fish fries on Fridays. It was catfish or perch, battered and deep-fried, so good!, and the price was right.

I remember when members of the Knights of Columbus would be out on the street corners wearing their yellow smocks that had large red or orange lettering "Help the

Retarded" and K of C. Those smocks would later be replaced with politically correct language that indicated the donations would go to help those people who have intellectual or physical disabilities. Even though the project had a complicated name, the consensus was always that the program was "The Tootsie-Roll Drive." Little Tootsie Rolls were given out to anyone who donated. The annual event was always well received in my local community, and I remember thinking that this was a good and positive K of C program. Little did I realize back then as a little boy, that a few decades later I would be wearing the same kind of smock and collecting for the "Tootsie Roll Drive." My father was not a Knight of Columbus. My immediate family had limited participation in the Catholic Church during my childhood years. Our community was predominantly Protestant, not Catholic. This may have influenced their lack of involvement.

I can recall at a young age our family going to Mass but not being involved with Church programs or ministries. As an employee of the university, my father could send his children to the private University School, where both my brother (Edward) and I would go. It would not be until I entered college and began attending a College Newman Center that I would become a "Practical Catholic." That term would have described my father's younger brother James. He was very active in his local parish and in the Knights of Columbus. While I learned this after Uncle Jim had died, I believe he was very active in his council, being that type of guy.

Coming up, Readers will learn how my Catholic Faith grew into a lifetime commitment of service, being destined to hold many roles in the Knights of Columbus.

CHAPTER 2

Finding My Catholic Faith

When I was about ten years old, we moved into a house near the heart of the university campus where my father was a professor and my mother a teacher. During my high school years, I preferred socializing with college students over kids my own age. To fit in meant becoming a fast learner and acting beyond my age. That social circle shaped my perspective on politics. The late 1960s and early 1970s were turbulent times. The unpopular war in Viet Nam spawned anti-war protests, sometimes even riots. College students were the most vociferous opponents of the war. A five-minute walk from

my house put me in the middle of these frequent and bois-
terous rallies.

I got to hear both sides of the controversy. I stayed on
the fence regarding the war in Viet Nam. I could not see the
point of sending young Americans to Southeast Asia when
it did not directly affect our homeland. Still, I strongly supported our troops and the honor, tradition, and dedication
they showed in defending America. I strongly supported
the anti-communist positions of our government.

My father had served during World War II, with the rank
of Pharmacist Mate in the US Navy Medical Corps. I am told
that he drove an ambulance and considered becoming a
doctor. But seeing the horrors of war up close, the blood
and gore changed his mind; he had seen enough for a lifetime. He returned from the war and entered college under
the G.I. Bill, finishing with a Ph.D. in Education. He rarely
spoke about the Viet Nam War, but he leaned conserva-
tively when it came to supporting our troops. I was proud
of his service to our country.

I remember playing chess with ranked players in the
student union, playing ping-pong and pinball games and
shooting pool in the billiard room. There was a room in the
lower level of the student center where many of the campus hippies and political activists would hang out called
the "Toon-Room." There I would often visit after school,
stopping to see and hear coffee house musicians, poets
and the like all talking about the issues of the day. It was
a fascinating period of time in our history, and it afforded
me a unique perspective in my education, to say the least.

On one occasion the lecture circuit featured Abbie Hoffman, G. Gordon Liddy and Timothy Leary; I had to see this
debate for myself. I got there early to get a close-up glimpse
of these three combatants. To my surprise, all three arrived in the same limo, talking and laughing as they made
their way into the building. That was my first glimpse of
paid politics. A high school friend, a military brat whose
father was an Army colonel, was also head of the campus ROTC program. I remember the Colonel's perspective
about the many issues of the day. It was in stark contrast
to the Toon Room students who supported the anti-war
rallies around campus.

CATHOLIC FORMATION

One of my sanctuaries was the Catholic Newman Center (Christ the Teacher Chapel), where I attended Catholic Mass. That is where I completed my formation process as a Catholic and received the sacraments of Penance, Communion, Confirmation and, later, Matrimony; it is where I learned the workings of the Church. I associated more with converts to the Faith. I found my faith not as a child but as a young adult. But it was my late wife who awakened my faith, to whom I will always be grateful.

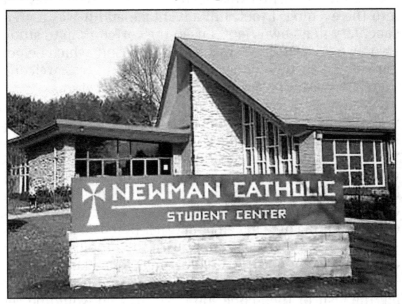

I became friends with the staff and the priests at the Newman Center. The pastor was Fr. Robert (Bob) Hoffmann, now a Monsignor. Another priest became a lifelong friend, Fr. William (Bill) McDonnell, now Monsignor Bill. He would be my principal confessor and one of the influential teachers in my faith journey. Fr. Bill would be the Principal Celebrant at my wedding and would later baptize our first-born daughter, Magen.

For those of you who remember Trans-World Airlines (TWA) and more specifically TWA Flight 847, on June 14, 1985, the flight was hijacked by Shiite Hezbollah terrorists. Unfortunately, U.S. Navy construction diver Robert

Stethem was killed and his body dumped on the runway. The passengers were held hostage for seventeen days; Monsignor Bill was on that flight. I recall many movie spoofs being done over the years, involving a priest and group of pilgrims. Well, he was the real deal and had been visiting the Holy Land with a group of parishioners when they endured that harrowing experience. Msgr. Bill, now retired, and I still exchange Christmas cards and update each other on the doings in our lives. Msgr. Bill is also a longtime member of the Knights of Columbus.

The Newman Center was open most hours of the day and into the evening. I took full advantage and it was a great sanctuary in its own right. I used the coffee shop to study. I would also visit the chapel and talk to God, which helped me cope with day-to-day issues. Everyone was welcome there, no matter background, race, or social status.

One day, a particular man just appeared, dressed in nothing but a tattered tunic. He was barefooted with long black hair and a long black beard. He went by the name "Prophet John." He carried nothing but a tattered Bible. He was always making notes and highlighting texts in the Bible, whenever he was not preaching or talking with whomever would listen. John would appear at campus events, either standing on a bench or another perch so he could be seen and heard. He blended in with the hippies and drew crowds of twenty or thirty, sometimes much larger.

On one occasion, we (Catholic students) were anticipating the visit of then-Pope John Paul II, who would be celebrating Mass in Chicago. People were making plans to go to see the Pope. Our campus was located about sixty miles west of the city, and transportation was by either bus or private car. Prophet John was looking for a ride to go to see the Pope. He wanted not so much to hear the Pope, but to share with him his message for repentance.

Our pastor, Fr. Bob Hoffman, was a very wise priest and used "Prophet John" as the topic of a homily. I still remember the theme of that message—how Jesus was treated by his own community. Though we all saw "Prophet John" as just a hippy who liked to preach, our pastor pointed out several facts: 1) Our Prophet John never claimed to be anything other than a man proclaiming the gospel; 2) Our

Prophet John did in fact quote directly from Scripture and did not deviate from or distort the message in any way; 3) Our Prophet John did follow the teachings of our Lord, Jesus Christ, taking literally the message Jesus gave to his disciples—to live by the means provided to him by those who took him in. His only possessions were the tunic and Bible, no money, nothing earthly. Our pastor told us "Who are we to condemn this man or call him a fraud? How do we know he was not sent to deliver this message to us?"

Prophet John disappeared one day, just as mysteriously as he had arrived. There was no sign of him ever again. I don't know if he made it to see the pope or if he had just moved on to another campus.

I do know, nevertheless, that he had a lasting impact on me regarding faith and conviction. He so believed that he was willing to give up all earthly possessions to preach the Good News, even when being scorned and ridiculed. There was always the one who needed his message, the one who would change his own life, pick up his cross and follow the Lord.

Reflecting back on my years as a high-school student hanging out on campus, I would leave the often-chaotic events, walk the few blocks back to my house and our normal midwestern household, to have dinner as a family. Our town was divided into two distinct groups, the University or "College People" and the town folk or "Townies." People from the town tended not to socialize with the people from the university and vice versa, other than the merchants whose bars and restaurants catered to the college students.

In the summer months of the mid-1970s, I was often one of the few remaining students around campus and was hired as the kind of catch-all general maintenance person: I cut the grass, helped setup for Mass, cleaned out offices and moved boxes and other things at the direction of the priests. It was a great experience, and the Newman Center remained a central part of my life.

I was married in the Newman Center Chapel on June 29, 1977; my wife's uncle, then Father Tom Miller, a priest out of Ohio, concelebrated our wedding with Fr. Bill as the principal Celebrant. My first-born daughter would be baptized there. There was no Knights of Columbus presence then at the Newman Center, but there was a local council in the town, which had one Catholic church, St. Mary's, among a dozen other denominations, including Lutherans; Baptists; Congregational; Episcopal; and LDS (Mormons).

St. Mary's was a traditional parish with a Catholic School on the campus. The parish's affiliated Knights of Columbus Council originally met in the church basement but would later get their own building, The "Tootsie Roll Drive" was always a big event for the local Knights, whose members wore the bright yellow smocks with the bright red lettering. They would take up positions at major intersections and would walk the car lines at each red light. I did not think about it much at that time, but later in my life I, too, would be joining fellow Knights of Columbus to collect donations for the Citizens with Intellectual Disabilities.

INTRODUCTION TO THE KNIGHTS

During college years, I took part-time jobs to cover school expenses and tuition, fitting them in around classes and on weekends. I also took night classes and worked full-time during the day. The next semester, I took full-time classes and worked part-time jobs. I drove a truck, worked as a bouncer, a night-manager at a restaurant, an auto sales rep, a teaching assistant (teaching lab sections), a night manager at a filling station, an apartment painter (summers) a cab driver (Saturdays) and a city/charter bus driver. I would take classes in the morning, drive a bus in the afternoon, work my shift at the station, and on Fridays take a second bus shift that ended at 2:00 a.m. Then, I grabbed a few hours' sleep, picked up the cab at 6:00 a.m. on Saturday morning and drove it until 6:00 p.m.

The cab company job was interesting. One never knew what kind of character one would meet next. I remember the old TV comedy show, "Taxi," with Danny DeVito. The writers of Taxi never met some of my customers—even more bizarre than the TV show's characters. The owners of the cab company (where I earned good money, mostly in tips on Saturdays) were both descendants of Irish immigrant families, Catholics, and Knights of Columbus.

John Leonard and Ray Farrell were partners; they ran the cab company as a family operation. Working for them gave the sense that they looked out for my best interests. They took a liking to me and I remember them asking me about my faith. I told them I was Catholic and attended the Newman Center Parish. Then they invited me to Mass with them at St. Mary's Catholic Church, which served the township's Catholic population.

Soon enough, I was drafted to help usher and count the collection after Mass. This continued until one partner said, "You know, you would make a good Knight of Columbus." He wanted to sponsor me into the Order. I would be interviewed with the Admissions board, and upon approval, I would participate in an initiation ceremony called a "Degree."

I was prepared to join the Knights of Columbus at that time in the mid 1970s. However, John Leonard, who invited me to join and sponsored me, entered the hospital and died a few days later.

John talked to me about the Knights, about what they did in the local community to help various charities as well as to contribute to the parish. My own father had passed away when I had just turned twenty years old. One might say John and Ray adopted me. They took the role of father figure, not an employer/employee relationship.

Not long thereafter, I graduated from the university and went to work in Chicago, eventually moving out of the area. I missed out on joining the Order at that time. I was entering the work force as a professional, and had a wife and a new baby to occupy my time.

I did, however, recognize the importance of protecting my family, since my own father had died unexpectedly and without adequate life insurance. I purchased several policies from a leading provider, but would later move all of my life insurance coverage to the Knights of Columbus.

RAISING A FAMILY

I moved my family many times over the next two decades living in Illinois, Wisconsin, then back to Illinois, on to southeastern Florida, then to northern Florida, on to

North Carolina and finally after 9/11, back to southeastern Florida. During these years I was heavily involved in international business which required me to travel out of the country for extended periods of time. My ability to volunteer for ministry service or to get involved with organizations outside of my family or business was very limited due to the extended travel.

However, whenever I was home and attending Mass at our parish, I considered getting involved with a ministry. I was called to serve but could not yet put a finger on what God was calling me to do.

In 2002, my family and I returned to the place where we had been most happy, southeastern Florida. Our youngest daughter Alexis "Ali" was entering high school and we enrolled her at the new Archbishop McCarthy High School, located in Pembroke Pines, Florida. We purchased a home in the local community so that she could be close and so that we could again belong to the parish community of St. Bonaventure, where we had been members between 1990 and 1995. Ali was in the first graduating class at this school. Our older daughter, Magen, was in college at Florida State University and would, later after graduation, remain in Tallahassee, working for Florida DOT and then the Department of Fish and Wildlife.

St. Bonaventure Catholic Church is located in Davie, Florida, a rural community west of Fort Lauderdale and winter home to many of the racehorses that run on the circuit. It's a large parish with about 7,000 families, a K-10 school, and approximately 90 active ministries. Our Pastor, Father Ed Prendergast, is the founding pastor and currently the only priest assigned to the parish. He has had help from retired or visiting priests on weekends, but for more than thirty-five years he has managed this campus himself. Our parish is also very diverse culturally, with many nationalities represented, English and Spanish being the two most predominant.

RECONNECTING WITH THE KNIGHTS

Annually, the parish has a Ministry Harvest event where all the ministries at the parish can present service opportunities to parishioners. On such an occasion I again encountered the Knights of Columbus. I had interacted with Knights at parishes we attended in different states. But I was still traveling frequently and did not think that I could contribute much. But now I was putting down roots. I had a successful business, my children were doing well in school, my wife returned to work in a major law firm, which is where she could best use her talents.

Life was good, but something was missing, I felt blessed by all that God had given me in my life and career and I wanted to "give back." So, on this particular Ministry Harvest weekend in 2002, I approached the Knights of Columbus's table. The Council had been established at the parish a few years earlier. The founding Grand Knight had been a member of a council in New York, prior to his retirement to Florida. His name was William "Bill" Braun.

William "Bill" Braun

Brother Bill had served in WWII in the Quartermaster Corps. He was responsible for inventorying and guarding the three atomic bombs, two of which would be used in Japan. After the war, Bill returned to civilian life working for the New York Post Office before retiring to Florida. Bill was the most active recruiter in the Council. He was quick to tell me the many ways that the Knights supported the parish and the local community. He asked whether anyone had ever invited me to join? I said, 'yes' and told him about John Leonard who wanted to sponsor me but passed away before I could take the degree. "Well, I am asking you now,"

Bill said, "Please consider joining us." I took him up on it. Bill directed me to the Admissions Committee. Two or three people on the committee interviewed me. Bill later called and gave me dates for the degree. But travel continued to get in the way. Several months passed. Bill maintained contact, giving me the next date of a degree, and was always encouraging.

Finally, a degree was to take place in a parish about half-hour from where we lived. That night I met Bill at our parish and rode with him to the degree. They put on both the First and Second Degrees that evening. I would forever be changed after experiencing the degrees. The lessons imparted came from a very good degree team and the words and delivery made a lasting impression on me. I also remember thinking how dedicated and focused the existing members were and how much they seemed to value the importance of the ceremony and of gaining new members.

I got involved with the local council and began to help out with the monthly Pancake Breakfast, the Parish Festival and other activities around the parish. I learned about the other degrees of the Order and, shortly thereafter, took the Third and Fourth Degrees. Through these degrees, Bill was always there to support me, and be the first in line to congratulate me at the conclusion of the ceremony. I never forgot how much I appreciated having my sponsor present for these events, and in later years I would make a point of always trying to attend the degrees of people I would sponsor to join the Order.

CHAPTER 3

Life Is Good

In 2002, I was still involved in international business, making trips to India twice annually, for about thirty days each. Most of these trips involved stops in Indonesia, the Asia/Pacific region, or the Middle East, on the way to or from India. I made seven round-the-world trips during these years. Each of these trips started and returned from the same point. I could not reverse my route but could make as many stops along the way as I wanted. These trips, while interesting, were exhausting.

During these trips traveling alone, especially on Sundays, I would seek comfort in a Catholic church or cathedral.

The architecture and local influences that each offered impressed me. My business in India was primarily with a paint manufacturer in Chennai in which I had part interest.

Besides my business in India and the Asia-Pacific, I did business in several Caribbean islands, mostly The Bahamas, but also Trinidad, Jamaica, Dominican Republic, Costa Rica and the Cayman Islands. My Caribbean trips were typically for a week at a time; with less time away from my family than with the month-long trips to India.

COUNCIL PARTICIPATION

During these years I devoted more and more time to the Church and the Knights of Columbus. My youngest daughter attended a Catholic high school where she needed service hours. I took her with me to pitch in on parish events sponsored by the Knights, such as weekly coffee service after Mass, monthly pancake breakfasts, dinners, and fish-fries during Lent. These were family activities. My wife would often join us to help, and later, my mother, who retired to Florida in 2006.

In 2003, with council elections for officers coming up, I decided that I would run for one of the guard positions to "get my feet wet." Well, that did not work out. As mentioned, the current Grand Knight was Bill Braun, who had launched the Council.

Bill had served two one-year terms, followed by a man named Dennis Mello, who also served two one-year terms. Then, Bill stepped up for another year. No one else seemed to be willing to serve as Grand Knight. Bill needed to pass the baton after six years; it was his time to do something else. Several members then told me that if I did not step up and agree to run for Grand Knight, they feared the council would have to shut down.

They said that someone with some "business sense" needs to take over; reluctantly, I agreed to have my name on the ballot and was elected the third Grand Knight of the Council. We had about forty listed members, of which fifteen to twenty were active.

SERVING AS GRAND KNIGHT

During that first year as Grand Knight, I learned not only what it was to be a Knight of Columbus, but also the inner workings of the order. Being part of a large 4th Degree Assembly (Michael J. Mullaly Assembly No. 157) had many advantages for a new Grand Knight. The assembly had 375 members. It was the largest in Broward County, Florida, and one of the largest in the Archdiocese of Miami. At monthly assembly meetings I met with other Grand Knights of area councils, plus other influential people such as district deputies.

In my first year as Grand Knight, we established programs officially sanctioned by the Supreme Council. One was the "Squires Circle," for young men aged 10 to 18, which prepare them to become Knights upon their eighteenth birthday. The Squires attracted boys who wanted to deepen their faith, learn leadership skills and have fun in the process. Squires service included participation and support for the parish school, plus various youth activities, e.g., recognition for the altar servers. At the State Convention, our council received first place on Youth Activities for our division.

During my second term as Grand Knight, we achieved the Star Council Award for the first time in our council's history. We were growing in membership and influence in the parish. By the end of my second year as Grand Knight, we had broken the 100-member mark and were attracting young families to join us. We began to get involved in district events, multi-council programs for youth and even the district-wide annual picnic.

As Grand Knight, I became a delegate to our annual state convention. My first convention was in May of 2003. The content of the programs, the quality of the speakers and the feeling of unity with my fellow delegates were all impressive.

The Convention sparked my first thoughts about a higher role with the Knights (perhaps my calling). I saw the men on the dais and wondered what they had experienced and learned along the way. By the second state convention, I imagined myself being on that dais someday. It was a strong urge to participate more fully and help this incredible organization reach greater heights.

There is great personal satisfaction in participating in the terrific charitable programs the Knights of Columbus supports. Close to my heart is raising funds to help the disabled, and to support local food banks and the local St. Vincent de Paul program. Knights' support for the Special Olympics is deep rooted and derives from founder Sargent Shriver's devotion to the special athletes who compete. My spirit was awakened (as his had been) and I looked forward to every event. Each time I participated in one of these charitable events, the peace and grace of the Holy Spirit accompanied it. When we bless others, we are blessed.

TOOTSIE ROLL DRIVE

On one occasion, I volunteered for a shift during our annual Tootsie Roll Drive or what would later be called the "Campaign to Support Citizens with Mental and Physical Disabilities." We obtained permission to solicit donations outside a local Publix supermarket, and I drew the Friday night shift. I could have been home watching a game on TV, enjoying an adult beverage and a snack. Rather, I tolerated the heat, holding a donations can, wearing a bright yellow smock that said, "Knights of Columbus" and "Help the Retarded"—words that do not fit well today.

My smock's pockets were stuffed with tootsie rolls, ready for the shift. On most nights during our annual drive, one could expect around $20 in donations—loose change, quarters, half-dollars and paper dollars, with the occasional $5 bill being a rare find. On this night, a tall man in his late 60s or early 70s approached. He looked at my smock and muttered "Knights of Columbus—what kind of group are you?" In my best practiced pitch, I said "The Knights of Columbus is the world's largest Catholic Lay...." He cut me off at *Catholic*. "I used to be Catholic! I have not been to a church in over twenty-five years." Then he walked into the store. All sorts of things ran through my head. Was he unstable? Why did he decide to tell me that he was once Catholic? He seemed agitated. What happened to him to cause his animosity?

After ten minutes, he exited the supermarket, with no cart, no bags, no groceries. He was heading straight for me with a determined look on his face. He got up close to my face and started asking me questions about the Church, about our politics, our positions on social and moral issues. I was caught off guard, thinking who am I to defend the Church's position on so many issues? I had no special insight; I was a typical parishioner. But he wanted my response. He wanted answers. I remember thinking that I could really use the Holy Spirit's help. I answered him as best as I could, but after several questions he walked briskly back into the store.

What had just transpired? Had I given a weak answer or said something that drove him off? Was he unbalanced and confused or just argumentative? Suddenly, he was heading my way again; the look on his face even more determined. He was not pushing a cart; he had no grocery bags, just a head of steam as though he was ready to fight. I braced for an impact, but he stopped short and began throwing more questions at me about the Church. These questions focused on faith, church precepts, what they represented and what impact the Church was having on our society.

I waded into places in my memory, long since forgotten. Yet, somehow, it flowed out of me. I sensed that it was not I who was in control. The Holy Spirit (as I had hoped) delivered answers. Yet, back he went into the store. Did I offend him or at the least, not given him good answers? Something was going on here. I started to trust the process. That is when the feeling of calm, an awareness of the Holy Spirit's presence, came over me.

Another ten minutes went by when he exited again. This time with bags of groceries. Ah, but now his walk was different! The look on his face had changed; it had softened noticeably. He approached closely, then stopped. He smiled and said, "I wanted to let you know that I am going to go to church this Sunday," and he walked off to his car.

Wow! When he said that he would be going to Mass, I knew the Holy Spirit had been with us throughout this encounter. It was an epiphany moment in his life and mine. When we do God's work, He's there to help; He leads seekers our way.

I took a few minutes to relive this experience. How unusual, how emotional, how surreal! For the interim, I had forgotten about the donations. Remember, we would typically take in about $20 in change. I was looking for some kind of sign, some validation that what I had just witnessed was real, was in fact the Holy Spirit. While that thought was passing through my mind, I began opening the donation can, to count the collection. Wow, again! There was over $180 in the can—unheard of but it called to mind the story about the "loaves and the fishes." While talking with this man, people had been stopping by and putting their donations into the can. I could not even remember handing out Tootsie Rolls!

God does work in mysterious ways. I could not forget that. It is one of the gifts of grace that I have received as a Knight of Columbus. There would be many more of these epiphany moments in the years ahead. Each is utterly gratifying.

GIFTS OF GRACE

On one occasion, I was invited to speak at the end of Mass, at a local chapel affiliated with the Schott Communities, of Cooper City, Florida. They support and train persons with certain physical and intellectual limitations. At the time, I was a District Deputy. I spoke with the director of the facility about the possibility of either setting up a council there or at least a "roundtable" an affiliation with one of the local neighboring councils.

The center originally had been opened with the intention of serving the needs of the hearing-impaired. Later it expanded to include others with various physical or intellectual limitations. Catholic Mass is said each week in its chapel; simultaneously, the service is translated live into sign language. I marveled at how the signer, standing at the side of the altar, presented the words of the celebrant in sign. Congregants were responding also in sign. It was another epiphany moment.

The sense of community filled my spirit at that moment. When I was called up to speak at the conclusion of Communion, I had a speech planned, but after witnessing the

Mass, I tossed aside the speech and spoke from the heart, I said to the congregation "I would like to thank you for sharing with me a great gift! The gift of seeing the gospel for the first time. All my life I have listened to the Word, but today you visually showed it to me through your participation in the Mass through signing."

Seeing the responses and witnessing God's word delivered uniquely, so different from my usual world, instilled the same awe and wonder that a new convert to the Catholic faith must experience. The congregants stood up, cheered and applauded. They sensed I had really tuned in to something special. No matter the limitation, no matter the disability, God cares. He finds a way to make known his Presence.

Such experiences have deepened my faith. I often reflect on them. I share them with others during membership rallies. It is the heart and soul of why we recruit—to share with others the joy that comes when seeing the Holy Spirit at work. I have conversed with theologians, scholars and members of the Church hierarchy on witnessing the workings of the Holy Spirit. I wonder why the Holy Spirit gave me a front row seat, on the stage where great validating moments have occurred. There is only one answer: God chooses whom He may reveal Himself to, we do not. Let us all be watchful, not to miss it; and when it happens be grateful for witnessing the awesome gift of grace.

CHAPTER 4

Patriotic Degree

For most Knights of Columbus, the history of the 4th Degree is very familiar. Originally, three Degree ceremonies—Charity, Unity and Fraternity—characterized exemplifications. The principal of Patriotism was added in 1900, around the time of the Spanish-American War. Catholics were increasingly populating American cities. Yet many Protestants and non-Catholics were concerned that new immigrants, especially from Catholic Ireland, would not be loyal to their newly adopted country (America).

To ensure that Knights would unify around their country, the Supreme Knight appointed a committee to establish and format a new degree. The committee drafted requirements for the Fourth Degree—Patriotism. Candidates must be a Third-Degree member of the Knights of Columbus in good standing for three years. They must show evidence of distinctive service to the Church, the Order, and the Community. Over 1,000 men took the first Fourth Degree on February 22, 1900.

Originally, membership in the 4th Degree was by invitation only. A candidate needed to have a sponsor, have served in his local council as a member in good standing, demonstrated his patriotism through involvement in the programs and activities of the council and have served at least one year in the Order, prior to petitioning for advancement into the 4th Degree. Today, the requirements for advancement into the 4th Degree are simplified to the point that any member who is a 3rd Degree Knight, in good standing, may apply and take the 4th Degree Exemplification of Patriotism.

In 2003, I took the 4th Degree at an Exemplification conducted at a Marriott Hotel in Miami. The hotel was located on Biscayne Bay, with a great view of the city and the Intracoastal Waterway. Many local Assemblies hosted hospitality rooms during the event. On Friday night, an "ice breaker" event helped orient and prepare candidates for the degree ceremony. During the ice breaker, local dignitaries, the State Deputy, District Master and the Vice Supreme Master were all introduced to the candidates. This build-up for the following morning was informative and motivating.

On Saturday morning, we candidates registered and were then escorted to an antechamber. Everyone was dressed in a tuxedo. It felt auspicious with all the men in the regalia of the time. I was proud to be part of it. When it was time to start the program, we exited the antechamber, paraded through the hotel lobby and rode the escalators to the ceremony's venue. In route were our wives and families, taking photos of the Color Corps and the candidates. At the head of the procession, a bagpiper played marching songs. It was impressive, unforgettable! The degree ceremony was profound and touching—a history lesson that should be taught in every Catholic school. Upon being Knighted,

I was extremely proud to call myself a Sir Knight. More about the ceremony below.

Following the ceremony was the banquet. Entertainment included a five-piece dance band which kept us all in a celebratory mode throughout the evening. Beautiful backdrops made for great photos with wives and family members. But it was the sense of belonging to something greater and bigger than any honor we had experienced before that has carried each of us through decades of Knights' service. Many of my closest friends today were in this same degree class.

The inspiration from that degree led to my involvement with degree work. First, I learned a part in the 2nd Degree; then the 1st; then the 3rd; finally becoming an Exemplar on the 4th Degree team of the Florida District. I truly enjoy being an Exemplar. Years later, as a State Deputy, I would be the first in the Order to offer "Live - Virtual Degrees" during the COVID-19 pandemic.

Topping the list of benefits my 4th Degree provided was the beauty in the lessons taught. The exemplars delivered their messages with passion, knowledge and skill. As I became an exemplar, I would learn the part and, importantly, the history behind it. I wanted to express the message as it was intended—factually, credibly and passionately. The Knights of Columbus affords amazing opportunities for Catholic men. Degree work is a prime example. I will continue performing degree work as long as my mind and body permit. These ceremonies always have a high impact on new Knights.

Getting involved at the assembly level enabled me to expand my network among Knights. I met the 'movers and shakers' of neighboring councils. The old 80/20 rule was alive and well in Knights of Columbus councils. I learned that rule in college: 80% of the work is done by 20% of the people, 80% of the time. A core group does the bulk of the work for the majority. The same faces attended monthly meetings and events, though total membership is many times the number showing up for meetings and events. Understanding the 80/20 rule was a helpful perspective as I moved through state officer ranks.

I held the office of Comptroller at the first assembly I

joined, Michael J. Mullaly Assembly No. 0157. This was before electronic records replaced manual paper records. The assembly had over 300 members. I manually mailed out dues notices, newsletters and membership cards. It was a learning experience and gave me an up-close look at how 4th Degree assemblies operate. Over time I held other offices including the top position as Faithful Navigator. While I was Navigator, the District Master, a friend of mine, Gary McLain, asked for my support. His intent was to form a new assembly in western Broward County, with some members from Assembly No. 0157. We carried out the plan and I served as its first admiral and Color Corp Commander.

Later I helped form another southwest Broward assembly. There also I served as Admiral, Trustee, and Color Corp Commander. This assembly (Archbishop Ambrose DePaoli No. 3218) was named after the first priest ordained from the Archdiocese of Miami who became an Archbishop.

Archbishop Ambrose DePaoli earned a doctorate in Canon Law at the Pontifical Lateran University. To prepare for a diplomatic career he entered the Pontifical Ecclesiastical Academy and entered the Vatican Diplomatic Corps in 1966. He was named a titular bishop and Apostolic Pro-Nuncio to Sri Lanka. Additionally, he was Apostolic Delegate to Namibia and Botswana and Apostolic Nuncio to South Africa. He served as Nuncio to Japan and Australia.

The assembly would go on to support many programs and charitable groups in the Broward County area, part of the Archdiocese of Miami. One of the benefactors is the Schott Community Center located in Southwest Ranches, Florida. The Knights of Columbus contribute annually to this private, non-profit organization dedicated to the hearing impaired and the physically or intellectually challenged in South Florida.

The center is named for the parents of Joseph J. Schott, Jr. who purchased its "home" in Southwest Ranches. As a state officer and later as State Deputy, I often requested the services of a Color Guard, part of the Color Corps, a strong visible and recognizable symbol of the order. Color Guards participated in Masses, Corporate Communions, conventions and meetings. They often presented the colors at major league sporting events; they marched in parades and attended dedication ceremonies and similar events. Participating in the Color Corps also strengthened my faith. It reinforced my feelings of patriotism as a Catholic citizen of the United States of America. I had found a role in God's Kingdom that called for my capabilities and service. I was at home being a Knight of Columbus.

CHAPTER 5

Rising Through the Ranks

After serving in my council as Grand Knight for two terms, I was asked to consider becoming a District Deputy. A previous District Deputy, Brother Thomas "Tommy" Thompson, in charge of my council, was a truly inspirational mentor to me. Tommy had been a master chief on a nuclear submarine. After he retired from the navy, the Knights of Columbus became a good fit for him, and filled a fraternal void. Tommy had a rather gruff exterior, but his heart was devoted to service. He was very active at the State Council level, the local assembly and on all Fourth Degree teams. Tommy worked with me on the

Third degree team that I founded in the southeastern part of Florida.

I do not know what Tommy saw in me, but he took me under his wing and would advise me on all matters concerning the Knights. While Tommy maintained this gruff outer persona, as I got to know him over the years, I came to understand him as one of the most compassionate and charitable members I knew, he also had a great sense of humor and would demonstrate it at the most opportune times. So, when Tommy let me know that the State Deputy would be interested in appointing me as a District Deputy, I was flattered. However, at the time he first asked me I was just nearing the end of my first year as a Grand Knight and I wanted time to see whether I could really accomplish something in a second year in office.

We, in fact, did accomplish much in the second year. By then I fully understood how the programs and processes worked, I had made friends with successful grand knights from other councils, through the 4th Degree Assembly, and I had benefited from this additional time. My council was able to nearly double in membership as we gained many new and active men with young families who wanted activities that would benefit and support them. We had initiated a Squires Circle, which had more than twenty youth participating in it. We had a successful program for support of many of the other ministries at our parish and our pastor was taking notice of the Knights of Columbus as a "Go-To" group.

As my second year as grand knight was coming to a conclusion, Tommy approached me again and asked if I would be interested in moving into the district deputy position, he also kind of hinted that if I turned it down again, that would probably be the last time that I would be asked. He also made sure to let me know that it was a great honor to be asked and an even bigger honor to serve; so, I said yes. The next step was to meet the State Deputy at the upcoming state convention.

I remember it very clearly, Tommy brought me up to the dais at the end of the convention when people were wrapping up their affairs, packing up all the materials left over and holding final conversations. There was a line of people waiting to talk with the State Deputy, who at that time was Robert "Bob" Read, who went on to be a District Master for Florida and who later would head up the Wheelchair program in our jurisdiction.

Bob had served in the Marine Corps during the Viet Nam war; he would, in later years, return to Viet Nam on a mission to deliver wheelchairs with the Knights of Columbus and the American Wheelchair Mission. Tommy and I waited in the dais line, then it was finally my turn to speak with the State Deputy. First, Tommy spoke to the State Deputy, who then looked at me and said, "So, Tommy says you want to be a DD. If Tommy says you are okay, it's good enough for me—congratulations." And with that I was appointed.

DISTRICT LEADERSHIP

I served three years as District Deputy. By this time, I had learned much about the workings of the Order and recognized that everything we did as a fraternal organization was dependent on having a constant flow of new (and younger) members entering our ranks. Of the six councils that I had in my initial district, two of them were inactive, two were disorganized and two were actively engaged in many of the activities and programs of our Order; but those two were not actively recruiting new members. I managed to help get the councils refocused on conducting their business meetings efficiently, encouraged participation of the field agents assigned to service the members in the district councils and I saw that each of my Grand Knights had a council plan to follow.

We made Star District that first year and each year I was the District Deputy thereafter. In my second and third years as a District Deputy I would achieve the highest recruiter award for the jurisdiction. I am proud of the fact that my district recognized the importance of constant membership growth and having proper succession plans in place, so that our councils would always have a steady stream of new men to step up and become the next leaders of the council. Officers with new and fresh ideas make a council strong and go a long way in helping to raise the visibility of the council in the eyes of local parishioners and in the communities in which they are located.

Districts are typically composed of four or five councils that are geographically located around where the district deputy lives. The district deputy also has his own council as part of the district. In my three years of service as a district deputy, my district was reorganized several times; this was due to growth in the number of councils within our state jurisdiction. I ended up with six councils, two of them were Haitian Mission councils that had been inactive or suspended due to lack of funds.

Going to the Haitian Mission councils became one of the things to which I most looked forward. Here in our midst was a thriving community of Haitian immigrants, who I believe were probably much like the Irish, Italian, Polish, German, and others who had immigrated to the USA back in the mid to late 1800s. They had in common the same issues of a language barrier, difficulty in finding work, housing, and schools for their children.

For the Haitians, the Catholic Church was the centerpiece of their family life. Every member of the family was deeply involved in the life of the local Church community. I saw faith in the form of a deep reverence for the Mass and an appreciation of what the faith community would provide each of them. I remember that one of the councils met on a Friday evening, but it could not get the meeting space until 9:00 p.m.; the meeting would then run until after 10:00 p.m. This was not exactly where and how I wanted to spend my Friday nights, but I would come to cherish these meetings as I came to learn about their culture and grow with them in their success.

I recall that one of the first meetings that I attended was held in their Haitian Creole language; so, for most of the meeting, including the "Pledge of Allegiance to the Flag" I was mostly clueless as to what was being said. So I decided to try an experiment: I said to the Grand Knight, Brother Sam Williams, that we could recite "The Lord's Prayer" twice, once in English and once in Creole. I would learn (read) the Creole version and they would learn to recite it in English. It worked, they were happy that I made an effort to learn how to say it in Creole and they in turn would say it in English. Helping them to acquire English language skills became part of our meeting structure.

Another thing we introduced was the concept of fundraising. I observed in the early days of attending their meetings that they would have only a few members present. At the end of the meeting they would ask for money from each member; this seemed to be a real deterrent for some of them and I suspected that this was probably one of the reasons for low turnout. I suggested that rather than shake down the members each month, they try to do a fundraising event that would generate sufficient money to cover their operations. They decided that this was a good idea; I then said that they would have to come up with a plan that involved things that they liked to do, things that they had the skills to carry out, and things that would interest their community to support.

The council officers came up with the idea of a dinner-dance and a play. They would prepare the food, have a member provide the music (DJ) for dancing, and they could get the drama department from the local high school to give a performance of their current play. The kids doing the play would receive tickets for the dinner and the school would receive a certificate of appreciation for their support. The event turned out to be a great success and everyone had a good time, and the council was able to cover its expenses for several years to come. I recall being one of the few people from outside the Haitian community to participate in the dinner-dance event. The Haitians even had a special event where the ladies could donate to dance with me. I am not sure how much that raised, but it was great fun. I learned much from working with the Haitian community and to this day I still feel as if I am part of their journey.

STARTING A BRAND-NEW COUNCIL

While I was a District Deputy, I had the opportunity to start a new council. I knew that there was a new parish forming in one of the fastest growing areas in the Archdiocese of Miami, that was the parish of St. Katharine Drexel in Weston, Florida. The founding pastor was beloved by the parishioners but, sadly, he became ill and died before he could realize the dream of seeing the church built. I met with then Archbishop John C. Favalora, the Archbishop of Miami, regarding the opportunity to open a council at St. Katharine Drexel Catholic Church and he had no objections. In fact, he told me that he had just assigned an Administrator, Fr. Pedro Corces, to take over and continue to work on the project to locate land to build a permanent Church. At the time that I was talking with the archbishop, the temporary church was located in a strip mall storefront. The Archbishop also said, "Fr. Pedro could really use the help." So, I made an appointment to see the new Administrator.

I recall our first meeting—Fr. Pedro was being bombarded by people coming and going, asking questions, and making demands of his time. I said to Fr. Pedro, "It looks as though you could use some help." Then I said that the archbishop had himself made that suggestion to me. I then went on to explain what the Knights of Columbus was all about and how we worked as local councils supporting the parish with which we are affiliated. I also explained a little about the workings of the Order internationally. At the end of the conversation Fr. Pedro asked "When can you start?" We agreed to hold the initial membership drive on the coming weekend. We were looking for a minimum of thirty-five members to institute the new council.

When the weekend of the membership drive came, I had my district warden, Brother Pasquale "Pat" Fittipaldi, with me. Brother Pat would go on to be a District Deputy in his own right and would institute St. Andrew Council in Fort Lauderdale just a few years later. So, on the date of the first membership drive at St. Katharine Drexel, we arrived early and set up our table and posted our signs. I was given permission to speak from the ambo at the end of each Mass about the benefits of membership in the Knights of Columbus. Then after the recessional, Brother Pat and I would be at our table in the "outer lobby." Now, I should qualify what the outer lobby was, because at this time the parish was meeting in rented space in a commercial plaza.

One of the first men to approach the table was a fellow who was on the church planning committee helping to raise funds for construction of a permanent church building. The man was Brother George Hayek, who would become the Founding Grand Knight and later one of my closest confidants along my way to becoming the State Deputy.

In this first meeting, Brother George asked many good questions and I vividly remember asking him about his business. He told me that he was in real estate, and I then recalled Jesus' consideration of Simon Peter, "upon this rock I will build my Church." I stated to Brother George, "upon this rock we will build a council." Brother George indeed turned out to be very successful as Grand Knight, achieving the Star Council Award during his term and helping to organize many great events that later would be paramount in fundraising and construction of the new church building.

St. Katharine Drexel Council 14212 has earned the prestigious Star Council Award many times in its existence. We went on to recruit many more influential and rising stars who would later advance to serve at the state levels in many programs and on many committees. There were several key individuals who joined the Order as charter members at that time.

I also recall on that first recruitment day a permanent deacon, Rev. Mr. Paul Brancheau; he did not approach but kind of gave me a slightly condemning look from across the room. I wondered at that time what that was all about; he would later explain it to me. Doing recruitment weekends, I would typically give an overview of the works of the Order (big picture) at the first weekend drive. On the second weekend drive I would focus on what a local council would do to support the parish, and on the third recruitment drive I would invite new members who had joined following the first two weekends to participate in the recruitment effort. Deacon Paul actually came by the table and picked up some literature after the second weekend, and on the third drive, he came up to me after Mass and told me his reason for the earlier dirty looks. It seems that his father had been a Knight at the time he was growing up and his impression of the Knights was that it was an "old man's drinking club." However, after hearing about all the programs and charitable works that we did in these times, he was willing to explore the possibility. Deacon

Paul joined the order and eventually he became a 4th Degree Knight of Columbus and very active and supportive of everything we did.

FORMING A DEGREE TEAM

As District Deputy, I saw the need to form a new regional Third Degree Team. One had existed in the county years before, but had later dissolved. At that time, a Third Degree Team did not conduct degrees in their local area; they traveled to a jurisdiction where members would not likely be known by any candidate. So, we established the "South Beach Knighthood Team" with about twenty-five members on it. The old degree involved many actors playing various interactive parts. Some parts were long and involved; others were short and simple. But the team members really bonded and became like family. We hosted an annual dinner for members and wives. Fellowship included sharing stories of past degrees—things no one outside the team would ever know or be allowed to discuss.

A District Deputy observes how each council has its own unique style. Each would attempt to outshine the other in some respect. I would later, as State Deputy, take advantage of each council's uniqueness by tailoring programs to each council's strengths. As the top recruiter in the jurisdiction, I caught the attention of some high-ranking Knights. One was Brother Doug Murray, who at the time was very involved in degree work and was a State Officer. Doug was the State Advocate when I first met him, and we became friends. His wife, Loraine, was really the guiding force behind Doug, much as my wife, Marybeth, would be the guiding and moving force behind me. As Doug moved through the ranks we would often talk about the future. I had a background in technology and had introduced a website to my local council. I talked to Doug about how an interactive website could benefit the State Council. It could include an activities calendar listing all activities around the state from just one location.

The year before Doug became State Deputy, he asked me to be the State Public Relations Director and to take over the State Website, consolidating all state marketing and communications under one umbrella; I agreed. We began ambitious plans to introduce some innovations during the Murray administration.

Sadly, in October of the year before Doug was elected State Deputy, his wife, Loraine, died suddenly. She had just returned home from a Columbiettes' meeting carrying a dessert for Doug, saying she had brought "sweets for her sweet," then she just collapsed into his arms and died. Doug was devastated, but, even in that dark and depressing time the Knights of Columbus was there for him. I recall that within hours of Loraine's passing, Brother Don Goolesby, now a Past State Deputy, would arrive to stay with Doug for some time. A Knights of Columbus Field Agent showed up to support him with an offer for financial assistance, and many more Knights and their families came out to help Doug in his time of need.

Doug went on to be a great State Deputy, surrounded by a team of dedicated members. We all felt the influence of Loraine in Doug's actions. She had written a plan for everything during their administration. Doug followed the plan as best he could. As a team, we made many improvements to the state website. We upgraded the communications processes that were used to reach out to the members of our jurisdiction. My friendship with Doug Murray lasted beyond his administration. Little did I know then, that I too would experience the sorrow and loss of one's wife, when my wife, Marybeth, would succumb to metastatic breast cancer during my term as State Deputy. I often confided in Doug (and other close associates) to help me navigate through the loss and extreme grief. Observing how Doug carried on, contributing at a high level, inspired me as I went through the grief of my loss.

ASSESSING THE "WHY"

Following the administration of Doug Murray, I felt that I could contribute more if I were elected to one of the state positions or "chairs." It was about serving—giving back—for which I had joined the Order in the first place. With some God-given talent and decades of business experience, I sensed that I could strengthen the State Council and help the jurisdiction move into the twenty-first century. A top priority would be recruiting the next generation into our great Order.

As a state officer, the bigger picture of what the Order represents comes into view. At its root is a focus on relationships. New State officers are suddenly recognized by people they have not yet met. I was approached by people who had followed my progress, who knew my work; yet I did not know them. As I advanced through the chairs, I became acutely aware of how my actions, words and deeds impacted the membership and those who might consider joining the Knights. Increased consciousness of the responsibilities of the office, of the need to be a good example, are crucial lessons for leading and attracting recruits who will take us to an even brighter future.

As a Knight, we never know when or where we may be called on to lend assistance. We pride ourselves in being prepared and in being impartial when asked to help. One example stands out. I held a position as Vice President of a division of an international engineering firm. Around 2010, during the recession, our company offices were in a building with some vacant commercial space available. An excavation company rented the space from us. Family-owned, several generations of the family worked in that company. I became friendly with the principal owners—I will call them Don and Helen (not their real names). We often found ourselves in the break room at the same time. Don was a storyteller. He knew Florida history, had camped in the Everglades, and had hunted, fished, and enjoyed the good life in the Sunshine State. Helen was an outgoing personality, every bit into that lifestyle with Don.

During our conversations, it came up on several occasions that I was a Catholic and a Knight of Columbus. I started seeing less and less of Don over time but would often see Helen and other employees of the company. It seemed odd when one day Helen came into my office, as this was the first occasion for her to come directly into my workspace. She looked sad and told me that Don was dying. He had been fighting cancer for years; in remission for a period, but it was back and Helen did not think Don had much time left. I offered my sympathy and asked if there was something I could do. She said yes. She and Don were raised Catholic but had been estranged from the Church for many years. Yet it was Don's wish to have a Catholic priest hear his last confession. He wanted a clean conscience as he passed on to the next life.

Helen said that I was the only practicing Catholic she knew and asked whether I could help her find a priest, one willing to visit Don at their home. Don was no longer able to leave the house and was too weak to travel. I promised Helen that I would try to find a priest willing to travel to their home. Helen and Don lived about forty miles from me. I was unaware of a parish in their area, so I called my friend Monsignor Thomas Skindeleski, who was our State Chaplain at that time. Later, after a two-year hiatus he resumed that role when I became State Deputy.

I explained to Msgr. Tom about Don's situation. Though estranged from the Church, it was Don's dying wish to have a priest hear his confession. Msgr. Tom said, "I will see what I can do. What is their address?" The next day Helen entered my office with a big smile and a look of sincere gratitude in her eyes. "Thank you for sending that wonderful priest to visit my Donny; he has made Donny so happy."

While Msgr. Tom was with Don and Helen, he learned that they were married just before Don left for military service. They had a hasty civil ceremony but never had their marriage recognized by the Church. Msgr. Tom blessed their marriage while visiting Don. Helen stopped by my office the next day; this time looking somber but with the same peace that she had shown the day before. Don had passed away the previous night. She was full of thanksgiving that Msgr. Tom heard Don's confession and blessed their marriage; She wanted me to know.

I let Msgr. Tom know of Don's passing. "When's the funeral?" he asked, "I will see if I can make it." He made it. On arriving he introduced himself to the local pastor and said that he had visited with the family prior to the death. The local pastor said to Msgr. Tom, "You know the family better than I do, so why don't you be the principal celebrant and give the homily?" Msgr. Tom did that and the many family members, children, grandchildren, friends, and coworkers present were amazed at the story of faith, of how much it had meant to Don and Helen to have a priest hear Don's last confession, to have their marriage blessed and to be able to accept Don's passing with dignity and grace. Msgr. Tom gave everyone present what they needed to hear, but most of all, his presence validated the importance of faith and maintaining that faith in our Lord Jesus Christ as the way to eternal life. Msgr. Tom did more for that family and community than words can describe.

As a Knight of Columbus, I witnessed true 'Faith in Action.' Msgr. Tom's selfless act to visit someone, though not part of his parish nor even a (practical) Catholic at that time, but asking for the Sacrament, brought the Church's role back into a family's life at a critical point. Msgr. Tom, representing Christ, acted on the request and the Holy Spirit delivered the desired results.

I will not forget that experience. It strengthened and validated my own faith. I often recount that story to others, knowing that it would not have happened without being a Knight of Columbus. This experience and others like it recurred often in the years to follow. Being men of faith, as Knights, we will continue to witness the Holy Spirit's workings within our organization. By the way, I saw Helen a few weeks later and she happily informed me that she was back attending Mass, in fact she was going to daily Mass!

CHAPTER 6

Elected Office

B y the spring of 2011, I had been serving in state level positions for more than five years. Initially, I served as State Public Relations Director and overseer of all communications processes, including our state website, where I was the voice and often the spokesman or "personality" of the jurisdiction. Our State Deputy, Doug Murray, was a great communicator; in fact, he would be on the phone with me often several times per day directing me to get out a new thought or idea to the membership, usually by email, often posting on the website and even by initiating phone-calls through a group of people whose job it was to contact people on lists. We used these "phone trees" as an effective means of getting out a message to a group of people.

SUCCESSFUL MEMBER COMMUNICATIONS

One of the early discoveries that I made as Public Relations Director was that a large percentage of our District Deputies, and an even larger number of our Grand Knights, shared their email address, many times with a family member. This sharing of email was often a problem, for if the intended recipient was not the person who opened the message, often the message got discarded, lost, or ignored. I also realized that most often the person reading the email was the member's wife. So, I decided to try an experiment. I would address the communication to the member, but I would write it as if it were to the wife. This experiment worked very well, especially when sending out information on upcoming events in which wives and families were invited to attend. Including the members' wives on communications also expanded my visibility around the State Council.

At the State Convention of 2011, I recall many women approaching me in the halls, at the events and gatherings, they would come up to me and typically say something along the lines of "they appreciated the communications I was sending out," or that they appreciated being noticed and included; most often that they appreciated the humor. I tried to inject humor in my messages that went out, such as "when you are packing for the state convention, be sure not to leave your wife behind; she would not like that very much and your homecoming would be something less than a pleasant experience" or "be sure to make your hotel reservations early, waiting until the last possible moment may result in your not being able to stay at our beautiful resort hotel; rather you may end up at the No-Tell Motel many miles away, this kind of action will not be appreciated by your wife and she will cause you to suffer much on the car ride home."

I believe that the wives played a part in my being elected to the position of State Warden at that convention in 2011;

wives can have an influence on their husbands, of this, I was sure.

STATE OFFICER ELECTIONS

The election of State Officers in the Florida jurisdiction happens annually during the state convention. We have five elected state officers, typically referred to as "Chair Offices," starting with the lowest or first chair, State Warden, then moving up to State Advocate, State Treasurer, State Secretary and finally State Deputy. The title of "Immediate Past State Deputy" is given to the living State Deputy most recently having completed his term of office; he remains on the Board of Directors for another two years. Our elections are held annually; however, traditionally each administration serves in two one-year terms successively.

The State Deputy may at his pleasure appoint additional directors; these appointments are typically reviewed by the Board of Directors, prior to being announced. However, positions appointed by the State Deputy expire at the time he leaves office. Our Board of Directors indeed includes several appointed positions including the State Chaplain, State Chaplain Emeritus, State Membership Director, State General Program Director, State Charities Director and, depending on the administration, could include one or two other key staff; however, only the elected chair officers are state officers. While campaigning is prohibited, the rules do allow each candidate to let the membership know that he will be running for office and that he would "appreciate the member's consideration." In addition, each candidate is allowed to make a nomination speech or have someone else who meets the qualifications, per convention rules, make the speech on his behalf.

In my case, I chose not to speak on my own behalf. I figured that if I talked about all the things that I had done as a Knight and the awards that I had received, I would sound like a guy blowing his own horn. I did not want to come off insincere, yet I thought that if I asked someone who knew me well enough to "speak from the heart," whatever the results, I would be able to live with it. For my nomination speech, I asked Brother Mark Lynn to speak on my behalf.

Mark was probably a better friend with my wife than with me; however, we had over the years become truly brothers. Mark's background is in education; he has a PhD and has been involved with education at the highest levels. Mark is also well-versed in all matters theological, often reviewing textbooks and reports of theology. Mark also has a wicked sense of humor; he has been known to keep a room full of Knights entertained with his rapid-fire wit for hours at a time. Mark would, on occasion, tell people how he had lost his own brother, who happened to be named Scott, and how I ended up being part of his life. So, in a sense God gave him another brother Scott.

When I asked Mark to give my nomination speech, he said "you may not like what I say; I tell it like I see it" I told him that I just wanted him to speak from the heart; whatever he wanted to say would be fine with me, and then it would be up to the membership to decide if they wanted to have me, or someone else, representing them. I ended up winning the election by a slim margin. I still believe the difference was due in part to the fact that I had someone other than myself give the nomination speech, someone who knew me well enough to talk about the vision I had for the state council. My worthy opponent, Brother Lorenzo Rodriguez, had chosen to give his own nomination speech. While he was very eloquent and most articulate, and had an amazing history of service, giving his own speech and probably holding back so as not to sound arrogant, probably did have an effect on the outcome. My choice of a speaker who could be free to say whatever he thought worked out to my advantage.

I also came away from the experience of running for state office with a deeper respect for the men who had come before me and an appreciation of just how special the honor to serve really was. Following the announcement of the election of state warden, Brother Lorenzo was asked whether he had any comments he wanted to make to the delegates, since it was a very close election. Lorenzo then gave a most magnanimous talk, and he made an offer of having all his delegated votes be recast to me; this was so that I would have a unanimous vote of support. I never forgot that kind gesture.

Brother Lorenzo and I were friends, having worked together in degree work for several years. He is a Cuban immigrant, who has contributed significantly to his adopted country. Brother Lorenzo has a booming voice. When he spoke, everyone listened. We shared similar goals and desires for the Knights in Florida. During that election, we pledged to each other that whoever won, the other would be strongly supportive. Later, when I became State Deputy, I asked Brother Lorenzo to be the State General Programs Director and a member of my board of directors.

SERVING AS A STATE OFFICER

Starting out as a newly elected State Warden began with a whirlwind of activity, immediately after the election. A traditional rite of passage was for the incoming State Warden to take possession of all the property of the state council, following the conclusion of the convention, even though officially he would not be installed for another month. I can remember loading a trailer with the property and taking it out to the storage unit, where the previous warden had kept everything. This location was five minutes from his home, but it was over four hours from where I lived. I would shortly thereafter rent a new storage unit near my home and move the contents of our state warehouse to the new location. I recruited two of my degree team buddies, Ron Brown and John O'Toole, who would later serve in high offices of State Ceremonials Director and Florida District Master, respectively. On the day to move the warehouse, I rented a truck.

We drove up and back in the same day which made for a very long day, a day that had started with an invitation to have breakfast at a restaurant managed by a Knight, Brother Rob Urrutia (pictured here), who would eventually succeed me as State Deputy. After loading the items and cleaning out the prior storage unit that was located north of Orlando, we headed back to Pembroke Pines, about a four-hour drive, where I had secured the new warehouse. Along the way a fierce storm blew in, and upon our arrival we were forced to unload in the pouring rain. I will never forget the experience; and having to unload in the rain just made it that much more unforgettable. The three of us bonded during that experience and have remained close friends through the years.

As a State Warden, one is charged with managing and maintaining all the property of the jurisdiction. The State Warden is also responsible for setting up and organizing state meetings and the state convention. At the time that I took over the position, all registration for our state convention was processed manually and by U.S. Mail. This required mailing out more than five hundred instruction letters, receiving the response to those letters, then mailing out the registration packets to each of the elected delegates to the convention. Then, after the delegates receive the packet, they must fill out the registration card and mail it back with a check for the items they had selected. Once I got that mailer back, I had to try to read the writing (sometimes easier said than done), then process tickets for each event they had selected, and then put the tickets into an envelope. The envelopes were then placed in boxes and arranged alphabetically and would be handed out at the convention.

It only took me one time to realize there had to be a better way. So, I developed the system to issue a barcoded name badge that included each activity that a delegate or other attendee had purchased, rather than printed tickets. The name badge served as the authorization. Delegates signed their name badge, so it also served as their official credential. The name badge also contained the most current photo of the member, to prevent people from granting access to unauthorized persons and to prevent the reselling of event tickets.

During my time as state warden, I also designed and had built a permanent altar to be used for the Celebration of Mass at official state council functions. The altar has a unique altar stone embedded in the top; under the altar stone is sealed a relic of our founder, Blessed Michael McGivney. The altar also contains some very old wood (walnut) that came from my family. My great uncle was an engineer with an icebox company; he also made cabinets. In those days the icebox cabinets were wood with lead linings. The wood was left over from his cabinetmaking shop and had been harvested in the late 1800s; so, we thought it would be appropriate to use lumber for our altar that was growing at the time Blessed Michael McGivney founded the order.

After two years as State Warden, I was elected to the office of State Advocate. The State Advocate, is the legal representative of the jurisdiction. He is charged with carrying out the directives of the State Deputy on matters of trial, as well as in acting as the liaison between the Supreme Council's Advocate Office and the local jurisdiction. This office was one of the busiest that I could remember, having nearly three or four issues come up per day. I quickly realized that many of the calls were about similar issues, and that if I created a Frequently-Asked Question (FAQ) resource, I could probably cut down on the number of calls to which I needed to respond.

I then put together the "Advocates Forum," which became active on the State website around the same time that the Supreme Council began to post the "Officers Desk Reference" on the Supreme website. The Advocates Forum on the State website was not intended to duplicate or replace the Officers Desk Reference; but it was intended to provide FAQ answers to localized questions that tended to pertain to our jurisdiction. This proved to be an asset and it is still being used in that format today.

One of the biggest takeaways that I got out of being the state advocate was from past state deputies who would tell me, "You will have to deal with this again, when you are State Deputy" and they were right. Many of the same people with the same issues continue to repeat history. I had to laugh when on the first day of my administration as State Deputy, I had to deal with a case that involved a member who had been in the same predicament six years earlier while I had been the State Advocate.

Moving on to the State Treasurer's position, I learned everything about QuickBooks® that I needed to know in order to process the thousands and thousands of checks that you have to write. While I had significant experience in conducting investigations and writing professional reports, which came in very handy as State Advocate, I had little experience in finances. I had not used QuickBooks in the past and had a steep learning curve in moving into the State Treasurer's office. Getting up to speed with Quick-Books was easier said than done; however, by the end of the first month I was 'up and running,' with few issues. I probably learned the most while serving in the treasurer's position, both in how much it costs to operate a jurisdiction the size of Florida, as well as how much money our members raise for charitable causes each year. This position was truly a great learning experience for me.

The next chair was State Secretary. I would be the fourth elected State Secretary to that position, as prior to the three men that went before me, our jurisdiction allowed the State Deputy to select his choice of secretary (then a non-elected position). The General Program Director was the last stop before a candidate ran for the State Deputy position. So, candidates would successively serve as State Warden, State Advocate, State Treasurer, and General Program Director (positions each typically held for two years) before running for election to State Deputy. Florida changed its by-laws to include the State Secretary as one of the elected positions, in order to follow most other jurisdiction formats.

The State Secretary functions much like the Financial Secretary of a council. He is responsible for keeping the official records of the jurisdiction as well as keeping the minutes of all board meetings. He is a member of the state executive board as well as a key member of the affiliated 501(c)(3) charitable organization, Florida K of C Charities, Inc. The State Secretary processes all vouchers and sends them on to the State Treasurer for check issuance. In addition, the State Secretary receives a receipt from the State Treasurer for all monies received.

The State Secretary in his final year of office, also has traditionally been given the ample ability to travel throughout the jurisdiction in order to meet with prospective members of his upcoming administration, when he becomes State Deputy. One of the things that I remember most about being State Secretary was getting to understand the relationship between the fraternal and insurance sides of our Order. I was familiar with our general agents and many of the field agent staff, prior to becoming State Secretary; however, I really wanted to understand the concerns and get the ideas firsthand from the agents themselves. At this time, there were four General Agents in the Florida jurisdiction.

I scheduled visits to each of the general agencies, meeting with each one during their regular meetings. During these meetings, when it was my time to speak, I went around the room and asked each field agent to tell me in his own words the most important things he thought the state should be addressing regarding communications between the fraternal and insurance sides. I also asked each agent what was the single most important thing they would like to see the State accomplish during the next administration. I then shared with them my vision for our administration. This concept was very well received by the field agents as well as by the general agents. Having established good communications and a rapport with the field agents this would later prove to be invaluable, especially during the Pandemic.

CHAPTER 7

State Deputy

On July 1, 2019, I officially assumed the office of State Deputy of the Florida jurisdiction. However, the installation for State Deputies took place earlier, on June 7, 2019, at St. Mary's Church in New Haven Connecticut. St. Mary's Church, birthplace of the order, had been in the midst of a major restoration project and had been closed to the public for some time. The building had suffered from roof leaks, resulting in damage to much of the ceiling plaster; and because of the damage, the entire interior of the building was covered in scaffolding. The Supreme Knight and Board of Directors decided that the experience of being installed at St. Mary's was so important that they decided to suspend the restoration project temporarily, remove all the scaffolding and reopen the Church, so that my class of state deputies could be installed.

Along with my wife Marybeth, I was installed as the 59th State Deputy of the Florida Jurisdiction, by then Supreme Knight Carl A. Andersen. A blessing was offered by the Supreme Chaplain, Most Reverend William Lori, Archbishop of Baltimore, from the very altar where Blessed Michael McGivney had so often celebrated Mass.

PERSONAL TRAGEDY

At the time of our installation, my wife had already been diagnosed with Stage IV Metastatic Breast Cancer. She was undergoing treatment and was determined to continue to live life as normally as possible. I had asked her early on whether she wanted me to step down from the many ministries and organizations that I was involved in; she said "absolutely not." She was always an inspiration to others around her, never complaining, never turning away from the many charitable causes that we supported.

Marybeth could have just said, "Enough was enough," but she always put others' needs above her own. She was not only committed to seeing that our term in office be successful, but that she would fight the disease with all her might.

My wife, in addition to being an advocate for maintaining her life in as normal a way as possible, while still having mobility, would use her baking skills as a form of therapy. There is no other way to describe my wife: She was a baker! She took great pleasure in baking and presenting home-made goodie bags of cookies, brownies, and other delectable items whenever the opportunity presented itself. Marybeth was especially fond of seminarians. We have a nephew, Matthew Byrne, now Father Matthew, who was in the seminary a few years earlier. She would often send him care packages of cookies and other goodies and Matthew would share them with the other students.

Word got around, and soon she decided to expand her deliveries to our Florida major seminary, St. Vincent De Paul Regional Seminary, in Boynton Beach. Whatever the holiday—Christmas, Easter, Valentine's Day, 4th of July, Thanksgiving, Halloween—you name it, she had a cookie for it. Marybeth also baked and delivered little goodie bags to the VIPs and State Board members whenever we had a meeting or convention. She would get a list of the hotel rooms people were staying in and then deliver the bags to the door, hanging the bag on the outside of the doorknob.

On one occasion, I remember hearing from hotel staff that a high roller guest had come down to complain about not getting his "Special Goodie Bag" upon arrival. It seems that he had noticed the brightly decorated goodie bags hanging on the doors of certain rooms. He thought her baked goods were part of the hotel's "frequent guest rewards" program! Marybeth always was thinking of others. She wanted to have nice events and meaningful speakers' programs, so that people would come away from our events knowing that they got something of value for investing their time.

Unfortunately, my wife would not live to see the second year of our term, succumbing to the disease on January 22, 2020. The cancer did not define who she was, but her battle and her quiet dignity gave hope to those who were also suffering from disease or other debilitating condition. I will never forget the words of our Pastor, Father Edmund Prendergast, during Marybeth's Funeral Mass, when he said that "she was a longtime dedicated parishioner, and always very supportive of the Church; but her greatest gift was coming to Mass each week, sitting quietly in the same pew where she always sat, showing us all that her faith never varied. Even when she lost her hair and became quite pale, she still came to Mass and received the sacraments." He said that this was a great gift to the rest of us on keeping faith even in the darkest hours.

Another priest friend, the State Chaplain for Florida Knights of Columbus, Monsignor Thomas Skindeleski, upon meeting her, instantly took a liking to Marybeth; they shared a common Polish heritage. Monsignor Tom would later become one of the few people that she would allow to visit her in the hospital, and later in hospice. Another priest friend, Father Frank Roof, would be one of a few, other than immediate family, that she would allow to visit.

On one of Monsignor Tom's visits to the hospital, at Jackson Memorial in Miami, a more than one-hour drive for him, I happened to be visiting when he arrived. I had just been talking with a technician that had administered an oxygen therapy session for Marybeth. The technician happened to be Haitian, and we had been talking about the devastation caused by the earthquake in Port-a-Prince (2010) and how the Knights of Columbus had been helping with relief efforts. I had mentioned our wheelchair distribution and also that we had sponsored a children's soccer team, made up of kids who had lost limbs during the earthquake.

The technician got really quiet then he told me that his own sister had been on that team. He went on to let me know that he would be interested in joining our Order. I then asked him if he was Catholic? He responded, "No, Baptist." So, I replied "okay, we can fix that." We talked a while longer and I found out that he was not a practicing Baptist, but he had been confirmed in that faith. I offered him an opportunity to explore the possibilities of becoming Catholic; he agreed to pray about it.

Monsignor Tom, had called me on his way in and, as I was leaving, we met in the hospital lobby. Monsignor Tom would make many more such visits to Marybeth during her many stays in the hospital. He even offered Mass on several occasions in her room with me serving; what a special privilege it was to have this wonderful sacrament for her during this difficult time.

On this particular day, Monsignor Tom had in his possession a first-class Relic of Saint John Paul II. He was intending to bless Marybeth with the relic. Monsignor was dressed in his priestly collar and carrying the reliquary of St. John Paul II. I thought of the Haitian technician and asked Monsignor Tom if he would be willing to try an experiment. I recounted the story of my encounter with the young technician. I then said to Monsignor, "would you mind going up to this young man, if you see him in the hallway, then ask him "are you the Baptist? If he said, yes, then tell him you were there to convert him to Catholicism;" Monsignor laughed and said, "I will do it."

The point of this story is that you never know when and where the opportunity to evangelize will present itself. I kept thinking that this experience was really a validation of the power of the Holy Spirit at work. I do not know whether he actually encountered the young man, but the fact that he was willing and that I had invited the man to consider joining us was just one more validation of how much the Knights of Columbus bring out the best in each of its members.

I know that on that day, the seeds of faith were planted in that young Haitian technician; it now would be up to the young man to determine whether those seeds were planted in "fertile ground" or not. I would look for the young man during my daily visits, but I never did see him again. On Sunday I would bring Marybeth Holy Communion. Often the nursing staff would observe our prayers and time with communion; some would ask about it and I would reply that "faith sustains."

In the beginning of our term, Marybeth was still able to participate. Our administration began with the installation of state officers over the July 4, 2019 weekend. We had gotten permission from our State Chaplain, Monsignor Thomas Skindeleski, to host the installation at his parish, Saint Vincent Ferrer, in Delray Beach, Florida. His bishop, Most Reverend Gerald Barbarito, Bishop of Palm Beach, was invited to be the presiding celebrant at the installation Mass and he had readily accepted. Marybeth was having difficulty walking by this time and we did our best to accommodate her.

The ceremony was the first one in many years that had been presided over by a bishop and all who attended it were complimentary on the experience. Shortly into the term our first challenge was presented: we were met with several hurricanes, some that would directly impact our jurisdiction and some that affected our neighbors. I had formally established a state disaster response team, with a trained and experienced disaster coordinator placed at the helm. In addition, we established regional disaster relief coordinators at each of our dioceses. The team came together and worked with the Supreme Disaster Relief staff on a number of situations that year.

Hurricane Dorian was probably the first real test of our new Administration. This storm sat for nearly a full week over the islands of Grand Bahama and Abaco in The Bahama Islands. The storm effectively destroyed all the infrastructure on Abaco and much of Grand Bahama. We had councils on both islands and the Church had a significant presence in both places. It was during the preparation leading up to the storm that as State Deputy, I began to communicate directly with the Archbishop of Nassau, Most Reverend Patrick Pinder. The archbishop himself was leading the cause for disaster relief coordination for the Archdiocese, and I was designated the U.S. contact for relief efforts on behalf of the Knights of Columbus.

The Florida jurisdiction of the Knights of Columbus consists of the state of Florida, the islands of The Bahamas and the island of St. Lucia, West Indies. So, having the State Deputy of Florida lead the communications efforts for disaster relief was part of the process. In the week leading up to the landfall of Dorian in the Bahamas, the Archbishop and I had regular communications including text messages, phone calls and email. Prior to the storm landing on the Bahamas, it was still predicted to have a major impact on the land mass of Florida, so preparations were being made in both locations. During the storm, we were able to communicate sporadically; usually through text messages.

After it became apparent that the storm had caused catastrophic damage to the Bahamas, and as it was becoming clear that the storm would not directly affect the Florida coast in a significant way, we mobilized our relief efforts.

Many of our local councils took part in humanitarian aid shipments, using private aircraft and private boats to deliver food and water and other needed supplies. At the State Council level, we immediately set up a Hurricane Dorian Fund and began to advertise for donations. We also coordinated with the Supreme Council to put together container-loads of supplies to be shipped to the Archdiocese of Nassau, who would then oversee the distribution to those in need. In total, some five shipments and tens of thousands of dollars were raised and sent in relief efforts. I remember making a promise to Archbishop Pinder that we would send a special workforce of skilled Knights to travel to the areas hardest hit, in order to help in the rebuilding process. The workforce would consist of as many as 20 knights who would stay for a week or ten days, working on churches, schools and other Archdiocesan property in most need. The work was being scheduled to take place in July of 2020; unfortunately, due to the pandemic, the work was postponed until conditions would allow.

Then in January of 2020, MaryBeth's illness took a turn for the worse. We visited her doctor around the tenth, and the doctor suggested that she consider hospice, which signified that her time was growing short. We talked about it and decided that she did not want to return to the hospital, or a rehab center, and that hospice would at least give her the best chance of pain management. Initially, in-home hospice care was scheduled; a hospital bed was delivered to our house. Her condition, though, had rapidly deteriorated to the point that in-home care was not possible. She was transported to a Catholic Hospice facility in Miramar, Florida, where she would depart this earth on January 22.

I recall the night very well. Marybeth's sister, Barbara Byrne, and my son-in-law, David Naret, were visiting with me. We stayed with her until about 10:30 p.m. that night. None of the visitors had eaten and we left to get some dinner and sleep. We had planned to return early the next morning. I got the call about 2:25 a.m. that Marybeth had passed; we then drove to the facility and said our last farewell. I remember that there was a family that had a son in hospice directly across the room from my wife. The son died just about the time that Marybeth did. The father of the deceased was in the hall and recognized me as the State Deputy, as he said he also was a Knight and so was his son. We consoled each other for a few minutes. It was at that moment that I remembered something my grandmother had said on the occasion of the death of her son, my father, back in 1976. My grandmother said, "a parent should not outlive her child." I thought of the tremendous grief that this father was going through; yet he still could bring himself to console me in my darkest hour. I offered my support to him and his family; it was another testament of the great fraternal bond between Knights.

Marybeth's funeral was held early in March. The pandemic was becoming the talk of all news stations and the White House was trying to assure that everything was going to be okay. At that moment, there was yet to be any travel restrictions domestically, and all churches were still open. Marybeth's Funeral Mass was celebrated by my nephew Fr. Matthew Byrne, with my State Chaplain, Msgr. Tom Skindeleski, and my pastor, Fr. Ed Prendergast, concelebrating. Fr. Matthew gave a very moving homily reflecting on his personal memories of his Aunt Marybeth, as well as providing everyone present with a sense of how much she had loved and been loved by all who knew her. Monsignor Tom shared thoughts and words of Marybeth's compassion and her willingness to serve. Yet it was our pastor, Father Ed Prendergast, who had known her for many years to be a dedicated parishioner, who said how much she had taught him about the power of faith, in her presence at the Mass up until the time she could not physically participate, that really struck home. Marybeth had truly demonstrated unconditional faith, even when it was obvious that no miracle would occur to save her from dying from the disease. She accepted the cross that had been given and carried it all the way to the end.

Just before her passing, while sitting with her, I could not help but think about the suffering she was enduring; how fluid building up in her lungs was literally drowning her and how this was the same fate of crucifixion victims. It then struck me that immediately following death to this world, she would be met by our Lord Jesus Christ, who suffered and died for us, who upon that instantaneous conversion from death to life, from pain and suffering to joy and light, would be there to welcome her into the eternal kingdom. That realization gave me hope and comfort. At the same time, I realized that the grieving had started long before, and that at this time, I should unselfishly be willing to let her go to the peace and joy of her new heavenly reward rather than wish that she remain with me in the earthly suffering of her condition.

In the weeks and months following Marybeth's funeral, I was grateful for the distraction that the demands of the pandemic put on me as State Deputy. I was trying to manage, on many fronts, the normal duties of a State Deputy, while trying to come up with innovative means of keeping our jurisdiction alive, since many businesses, organizations and operations were closing. One of the earliest occurrences was the announcements of churches being closed. Since Knights of Columbus are practical Catholics and as such are accustomed to attending Mass at least weekly (Sundays) and on Holy Days of Obligation, the closures were having a very negative effect. Dispensations offered by the Ordinaries of Catholic dioceses, to wave the obligation of attending Mass in person, did help. But there is no substitute for the sacrament of Holy Communion, and I know that for all who were denied during the pandemic, the opportunity to receive Communion, it must have been a very lonely time.

I was truly fortunate in that Monsignor Skindeleski had offered to let me come to Sunday Mass at his parish, for the purpose of streaming the Mass over our State Media. I would bring the camera equipment, set up and stream the Mass, usually celebrated by Msgr. Tom and sometimes several other visiting priests. In addition to me, there usually was a few others present; the Music Director, two nuns and the parish videographer, as well as a seminarian who was present on several occasions, and a deacon. But that was it; we were the only people in the church. Following Mass, I was usually invited to stay for Sunday dinner in the rectory, with Msgr. Tom and the visiting clergy.

This was a special time for me, in that being alone in my house with no family nearby, and being invited to Sunday Mass and then dinner was the highlight of my week. This went on for many months, until the dioceses began to allow churches to again open with live, in-person Masses. I still have fond memories of those Sundays in the middle of the pandemic. My most favored memory is that I was never denied receiving Holy Communion. I feel so blessed and fortunate to have been able to do so and I constantly prayed for all those who were not able to be so fortunate, that they too would soon be able to again receive that most precious sacrament.

CHAPTER 8

The Pandemic

M arch of 2020 really marked the beginning of the pandemic as a real and present threat. Many businesses were closing their public spaces, such as restaurants, theatres, and places where large groups would normally meet. Other businesses were transitioning to what they thought would be temporary operations, and still others were preparing plans for how to survive an extended shut-down or closure.

The Knights of Columbus is a two-fold operation with the business side (Insurance and financial products) operating out of a brick-and-mortar centralized corporate structure.

Most operations were directed through staff located at the headquarters in New Haven, Connecticut. Field Operations were less centralized, with local General Agencies in each jurisdiction either having a fixed office and some staff, or working out of home offices. Most of the field agents work from home, however.

CHALLENGES TO OUR BUSINESS OPERATIONS

Up until early 2020 the typical appointment for a field agent, to talk with prospective (new) clients or existing members about their needs for new or additional products, was typically conducted in the prospective member's home. This process was ingrained into the standard appointment-setting process; in that after the initial contact was made and it was established that the prospect had an interest in hearing about the products available (namely life insurance, disability insurance, and annuities), the appointment was scheduled with the prospect. And (if he was married), with his wife. Most appointments were conducted during evening hours and during the work week. So, when the pandemic forced closure of most commercial businesses and made in-person meetings impossible, the Knights of Columbus had to come up with a safe transition plan that would allow for its business operations to continue. This mandated that a centralized operation of nearly 1,000 employees had to transition within a few weeks to a "work from home" format.

The enormity of this situation was unparalleled. For many employees new equipment had to be purchased, issued to the appropriate staff and set up. The requirements to remotely operate a huge financial operation were extremely challenging at best, yet the Knights of Columbus is an amazing assemblage of talent, and within a very short time all but a skeleton crew of essential staff were working out of their homes.

For the field agents, the transition would be even more profound. The traditional method of setting up appointments to meet clients in person, at the prospective client's house, was not going to be possible. Virtual appointments were going to become the new way of doing business. The virtual meeting platform quickly became the accepted norm, and most people seemed to adapt to this format within a reasonable amount of time. So, the long and short of it was that the insurance and financial side of the operation, in a matter of a few weeks, had made the transition.

CARRYING OUT OUR FRATERNAL MISSION

The fraternal mission side of our operation was a little different. Most communications between the Supreme office and local jurisdictions had already been conducted, for the most part, electronically or virtually. Communications often were transmitted via email or, in some cases, by fax; and in most cases, elected state officers, directors and volunteers who regularly communicate with the head office typically worked out of their homes, and were already used to communications via electronic means, email, and phone. Some issues that had to be overcome dealt with the processing of paper forms and materials which, in the past, would be sorted and distributed in the headquarters building by the appropriate staff; now this process would need to be sorted and sent out to people who would be working from home. This added a step to the process and, as could be expected, delays occurred in processing. Even with minor setbacks, the operation of both the insurance, financial and fraternal operations were able to continue with little disruption of service.

The state jurisdictions and specifically Florida, with which I was most familiar, would be a different situation. The Florida jurisdiction, consisting of the state of Florida, the islands of the Bahamas and the islands of St. Lucia in the West Indies, has a little over 55,000 active members. The jurisdiction had, at that time, approximately 360 active councils and over 60 active 4th Degree assemblies. At the time of my term as State Deputy, Florida had 88 Districts, each having a District Deputy and usually a District Warden to oversee between four and six local councils.

The Florida jurisdiction is composed of the Archdiocese of Miami, with the Dioceses of Palm Beach, St. Augustine, Pensacola/Tallahassee, Orlando, St. Petersburg and Venice and the Archdiocese of Nassau, Bahamas, and Castries in

St. Lucia, West Indies. Each diocese has a Florida K of C Regional Administrator who acts as the liaison between the diocese and the jurisdiction. Each Regional Administrator also has the responsibility of overseeing the activities of the District Deputies, who have councils located within each of the dioceses.

ORGANIZATIONAL MODELS

Traditionally, administrations had the leadership and other state volunteers attend two in-person organizational meetings and one annual convention. Training programs were scheduled and administered during those in-person sessions. There were also training programs and seminars offered via the Supreme training portal, as well as some training offered through the state and supreme websites. Regular communications and meetings between District Deputies and the State Deputy and other leaders were historically limited to in-person training sessions and in-person meetings. Often many months would go by without a district deputy communicating directly with the state leadership. This situation was due in part to the large number of districts involved and limited resources.

I, as State Deputy, was determined to improve upon this communications situation, and so beginning with the first Saturday of July 2019 and continuing for my two years as State Deputy, on the first Saturday of every month we held a virtual leadership meeting. It took place between 8:00 a.m. and 10:00 a.m, and usually had approximately 150 in attendance. The meeting was intended to put the leadership (State Deputy, state officers and directors) directly in contact with the Regional Administrators and District Deputies on a monthly basis. During the virtual meetings, we discussed performance during the previous month, we talked about the areas where we were doing well and let the DDs share success stories of "best practices." We also reminded those who were not active of the importance of adhering to the process and continuing to work through issues, so that they, too, could be successful.

I believe that having the monthly meetings every first Saturday, gave the leadership the consistency they needed, and it prepared them to stay focused on the work to be done. They all knew that if they did not show positive activity over the previous month that they would have to answer why their prior efforts were not successful. The district deputies who were following the program and were seeing positive results would be rewarded and praised for their efforts. So, when everything began to close down in the spring of 2020, we had already been successful in conducting virtual meetings. We had a platform that was in place, we had a process and procedure for using it and we had trained our people on how to connect, use and participate in on-line meetings. This was a distinct advantage and very important in our early abilities to transition to virtual operations and virtual degree work.

"Thinking outside of the box," of which this catchphrase has its origins in the following: The "thinking outside the box" phrase was popularized in part because of a nine-dot puzzle, which John Adair claims to have introduced in 1969. Management consultant Mike Vance has claimed that the use of the nine-dot puzzle in consultancy circles stems from the corporate culture of the Walt Disney Company, where the puzzle was used in-house. The origin of the puzzle comes back to Christopher Columbus' 'Egg Puzzle' as it appeared in Sam Loyd's "Cyclopedia of Puzzles" The nine-dot puzzle is much older than the slogan. In the 1951 compilation, "The Puzzle-Mine: Puzzles Collected from the Works of the Late Henry Ernest Dudeney," the puzzle is attributed to Dudeney himself. Sam Loyd's original formulation of the puzzle entitled it as "Christopher Columbus' egg puzzle." This was an allusion to the story of the Egg of Columbus. [wikipedia.org] The long and short of the subject was that it was only possible to solve the puzzle if you connected the dots from outside the square or "outside the box," thus using non-traditional methods to solve what normally would have been a confined problem.

CEREMONIALS: EXEMPLIFYING OUR TENETS

Back to innovation and thinking outside of the box. Early in the 2019 fraternal year the Supreme Council announced that the new degree of Charity, Unity and Fraternity would be introduced, and that eventually this new combined ceremonial would replace the old individual 1st, 2nd and 3rd Degrees of the Order. The individual degrees had been in use in one variation or another, for much of the history of the Order. The primary theme in all the older versions was "Secrecy," in that only a current member, in good standing, who had received the equivalent degree, and the candidates for that degree, were permitted to attend. All ceremonials were live, in-person events.

With the introduction of the new combined Charity, Unity and Fraternity (CUF) degree, the need for secrecy was eliminated and wives and family members of candidates were permitted for the first time, to watch the proceedings. This new degree would prove to be the game changer for the Order; it provided the ability to continue to recruit during the pandemic. Were it not for this new degree, our recruitment efforts would have been dead in the water! I truly believe that Blessed Michael McGivney had a hand in the timing of this significant change in our ceremonials, for shortly after the change everything shut down and live, in-person degrees would not have been possible again for more than a year.

The Supreme Council put out a video production of the new CUF Degree and was making this recorded degree available to on-line candidates. At first, there were only a few showings of this video but, as it became more and more obvious that the pandemic would not be going away anytime soon, the new video degree became the only means of getting a candidate into the Order. Florida, already using the virtual platform for conducting its monthly leadership meetings was the first jurisdiction to offer live, virtual degrees. We decided that the experience of actual participation outweighed the need to just offer a presentation that could be watched but not participated in. I also remembered how important it was to me, when taking my degrees, that my sponsor and fellow council members were present to congratulate me upon joining the Order.

I wanted to capture the essence of what new members got out of live participation, trying to incorporate that into a live, virtual presentation. Our plan was to create a virtual experience that combined as many of the "in-person" actions as possible into a live-streaming event. As the State Deputy, I saw the opportunity to be able to personally address, at its conclusion, each new member taking the degree. We decided that the best way to move ahead was to create regional degree teams who would be well-versed, practiced, and able to deliver the message of the degree with professional skill. These regional teams would use virtual live streaming from a central location or in some cases, where each member did his part remotely; and the overall ceremonial would be viewed by candidates either in a group setting or individually in remote locations. In many cases there were cast members from the former (3rd) Degree teams, located in regional areas; they became the core members of the new teams.

During the presentation, we would also encourage all the candidates who were participating from their homes online, to try to follow our instructions so that when we asked candidates to "break the fiber," each of the candidates in his own home would have previously located a piece of fiber that they could break at the appropriate time. We also encouraged the candidates to have a rosary nearby so that, at the appropriate time, the candidate could participate in the rosary placement portion of the ceremony. If there is a wife or family member present with the candidate, we suggest that they place the rosary on the candidate's folded hands.

Following the conclusion of the degree ceremony, which usually takes no more than thirty minutes, I, as the State Deputy would be introduced via the ceremonial team's captain. I would then congratulate the new members and any wives present, I would welcome each by name, parish, and council affiliation. This was something that had been done in the old degrees in-person, and was a way to make the new members feel included and special. I would watch the expressions on the faces of the new members and their wives or families when their loved one was mentioned by name. Often when I acknowledged the wife of a new member, she would be so excited to be recognized, that she would shout out loud. My message was usually short and to the point: I would remind the new members of the significance of the times in which they were joining and of how much the Church is depending on the Order for support during the pandemic. I would also ask them to meet with the financial advisor in order to get the most out of their membership, and to become active in their council.

Another thing was for me to remind them to consider inviting a friend or relative to join the Order. This would help us to continue our mission and would also help them qualify for the Shining Armor Award, an award given out to new members during their first year of membership, for achieving a number of milestones. After concluding my message, we would typically invite the new members to stay a few minutes longer, as we would play one of the "Into the Breach" series videos or something similar.

I mentioned earlier that our virtual degree teams were put together mostly from men who had previously been involved with ceremonial degrees of the older style. These men were used to memorizing lines, projecting their voices, and dramatizing for effect. We initially had four; then it jumped to six regional teams conducting the degree. The teams rotated through the month, so that on any given Thursday one of the teams would be the host. We also had a team that conducted a live-streaming degree in the Spanish language.

A NEW METHOD OF MEETING

The live virtual degrees proved to be a great tool for continuing to bring new members into our local councils; it also was a rallying event for council members to participate with their brother knights in something positive. Another virtual concept that Florida pushed was for local councils to move to virtual meetings. Even though this concept was also being promoted by the Supreme Council, there were limited guidelines and instructions on how to best accomplish this task. Florida was proactive in developing formats, and suggested scripts for councils to follow. We even suggested that councils consider having social virtual meetings so that they would have a chance to stay in communication with the council's member families. In many cases, the social meetings even included virtual games like a scavenger hunt or a game asking trivia questions related to a parish or the local council. Families and especially children were encouraged to participate in these social virtual events.

Florida was one of the earliest jurisdictions to utilize hybrid forms of the primary meetings required (by Supreme) to take place each year. The primary meetings are the Organizational meeting in July, the State Convention and the Mid-Year meeting, (typically in December). During the pandemic, we were limited to the number of people who could be present in a closed room, so we developed a hybrid format that allowed for many to participate virtually and for some to participate in-person.

The Supreme Council researched platforms that would be conducive to our needs. They developed formats and provided the scripts needed to conduct basic virtual meetings; the remainder was up to the individual jurisdictions to conduct the meetings. Florida contracted with a media production company to provide a live-stream, live-edited product. Our presentations included video of the live meetings as well as a mix of prerecorded material to complete the presentations. The result was that the Florida jurisdiction, again, was innovating and "thinking outside of the box."

By early May of 2020 we were well on our way to conducting virtual/hybrid meetings, conducting virtual (live) ceremonial degrees and promoting local councils to conduct virtual meetings. This was a great initial step, however, that alone would not be enough. We had to get down in the trenches and reach directly to the council officers, get them to buy in to the concept of keeping things going during the pandemic. We did have some councils that just decided that it would be too much trouble for their members to try to stay active; often this was associated with parish-based councils where the parish had closed off all buildings for any kind of meeting or public gathering.

During this early time, the Supreme Council came out with the "Leave No Neighbor Behind" program and began to identify knights and councils that were actively participating. Florida actively adopted the program and began to see some excitement from local councils that were able to do something during the pandemic that could help their neighbors, fellow parishioners and others in the communities in which they were located; this was truly a blessing!

The Pandemic was first reported in early 2020 by major news outlets and social media. Early assurances by the federal government seemed to indicate that this would be a short-lived situation and that "things would be back to normal in a few months." As the pandemic continued to grow in magnitude and scope, it was becoming clear that things would not be normal anytime soon.

One of the issues that I was concerned about involved the contract that I had entered into on behalf of the Florida State Council with the hotel that would be the site for our state convention. In order to secure dates and lock in room rates, food costs and related items, these contracts are negotiated years in advance. The contracts often include penalties for cancelation of an event; the closer to the event date, the higher the penalty. Our contracts contained such specific language that the penalty could have been $100K. I had several discussions with the hotel, and they finally agreed to waive the penalty, in light of concerns over the pandemic. This decision was appreciated by all of us, including the hotel management. We promised to bring further events to their property at some future date. Several months later, the pandemic would cause the hotel to close its doors and send its staff home.

Our organization, however, requires that we have an "Annual Meeting" or State Convention each year, so for the 2020 Annual Meeting, the Supreme Council came up with a virtual platform in which a streamlined business session would be conducted via telephone conference system. This system proved to be effective and allowed the delegates to the convention to be present via telephone. A company that specializes in conducting these kinds of meetings was contracted and the meeting was set. Our platform for the 2021 state convention included both accommodations for live attendance at the venue as well as virtual attendance by both delegates and any viewer who wanted to participate in the "open" sessions. Our production was streamed live on our YouTube Channel, Florida State Council Knights of Columbus, and included a "color commentator" desk that previewed upcoming speakers, conducted interviews of notables attending the convention and provided post-segment commentary. This production was first of its kind and provided the viewers and delegates participating at home a sense that they were part of the event and not just watching it on TV.

While coming up with hybrid forms of meetings and conventions was certainly a means of keeping our jurisdiction operating, what we did not appreciate at that moment was how much work it would be to do a production quality live-stream event. In our traditional format for conducting live in-person meetings and conventions, there was a loose agenda that was followed; however, there was always room for adjustments and questions and answers; often the presentations tended to wander off the agenda altogether. But in the live in-person meetings, we always managed to end at a fixed point in time.

Chaplain with Officers and Staff with wives
at the (hybrid) Florida State Convention, 2021.

Under the virtual or hybrid format, strict adherence to a scripted agenda would have to be followed. This resulted in many hours of planning and refining of scripts so that speeches would run in their allotted time slot. Prerecorded videos had to be checked for run-time and carefully scripted for their slots and the live commentary desk had to be ready and able to fill empty time and/or shorten or adjust their scripted segments to keep the scheduled presentations on track.

This new format of virtual programing had to be figured out and the appropriate staff appointed to the new positions. We also determined early on that we did not internally possess either the equipment or the expertise to conduct all the parts of a live-streaming broadcast event. After reaching the conclusion that we needed professional help, we selected several of our own state volunteers with media, television and live-stream credentials and experience, to head up our group. From them and with input from the various presenters, state officers and directors, the plan would come together.

An outside production company was chosen to provide the equipment, camera operators and technical direction. This would prove to be a great way to achieve our goals of "leaving no member behind," ensuring that we had a high-quality production and that should there be any issues, we had accountability through the vendor to ensure that any issues would be taken care of. Going forward, I assume that a combination of virtual and live events will be the norm. We will always remember that prior to the Pandemic of 2020, there never had been a virtual convention; but following the pandemic these methods will continue to be used in one form or another.

CHAPTER 9

More Virtual Solutions

I mentioned earlier that we had initiated the use of virtual meetings at the beginning of my term as State Deputy. Having come from a technical background (industrial engineering technology) and having prior experience participating in virtual meetings, webinars, and presentations in the past all contributed to my understanding of the workings of this kind of communication process and provided a roadmap for adopting these technologies and methods for our local councils to follow. In most cases, local councils that had been established for many years or decades had by-and-large followed a standard format that seemed to work for them. Most of these councils were strongly influenced by the local parish or parishes that were affiliated with them.

RECRUITMENT PATTERNS

New members had usually been recruited from the local parishes and often were sons and grandsons of current members (with cousins and close friends also being the most recruited), often referred to as "legacy members." Initiation ceremonies (First Degrees) were typically conducted by the local council's degree team, often by senior members of the council who had performed the ceremonies many times and had committed to memory the parts that they played.

Recruitment typically was word-of-mouth; in many cases a member would invite a prospect to consider joining the Order only after getting to know the prospect. It would often take persistence, with the member asking the prospect several times before the prospect would be willing to join. The member doing the asking would be called the "proposer" or "sponsor," and he would be expected to attend the prospect's degrees and to guide this now-new member along his journey as a Knight. This sponsoring of new members proved to be a method that would assure that he becomes active and accepted by the council, most often resulting in his success as a member.

The COVID-19 Pandemic changed the way we conducted the degrees; it also altered the proposer or sponsor process as well. This was a difficult area to overcome, but we had to again figure out a way for the proposer or sponsor to stay in contact with new members even when no physical, in-person meeting was possible. We came up with the idea of virtual social meetings, encouraging every council to establish a virtual meeting presence, schedule a monthly meeting and invite all members and their families to join the meeting.

Even if the meeting only lasts 30 or 40 minutes, it is a chance to recognize the new members who joined since the previous month, it gives everyone an opportunity to just say "hi," and to see the faces of others in the group.

Often many councils would include birthday greetings for those members who had a birthday during the previous month; in some cases, councils provided virtual games— such as a trivia question and answer game or a scavenger hunt for kids.

These social virtual meetings helped to keep the council members in touch with each other and provided a means of checking on each other. When it was noted that someone was missing, a member would be asked to make a call (offline) just to check on their well-being. Social meetings, using virtual platforms, work, but you still need to have an outline of what you want to accomplish, and you need a moderator who can keep it moving. In some cases, councils had few returning members to these meetings, I attribute declining participation on a lack of planning and poor moderation. For most, the meetings that were well planned, and well run, saw continued success and growing numbers of participants.

NEW TOOLS FOR REACHING OUT

Another benefit of the move to virtual meetings and training programs during the closure of meeting places was the ability to reach many people at relatively low cost, and to be able to schedule meetings at times of the day that normally would not be possible. Virtual meetings, in which the participant is joining from his own home, can be done after normal business hours, since the person does not need to travel to or from a meeting location. The result: many new training programs have been developed and implemented that take advantage of this method of communication and learning.

I am certain that many of the processes, technologies and methods used to continue operations during the pandemic, will be continued long after life returns to a more open or physical setting. This is the evolution of technology as well as the evolution of our society's acceptance of the "New" normal business practices; it will continue to evolve in the future, and the Knights of Columbus will continue to be at the forefront of technology, using it wisely to promote our Catholic norms and values. This combination will continue to serve us well as we move forward into the "new normal" of life after the pandemic.

The pandemic has taken a significant toll on membership. I can personally account for at least twenty people who have died since the pandemic first became apparent, many of them were very close to me, or were persons whom I had known for many years. Over a two-year period starting in January of 2020, I attended twenty funerals. I saw firsthand what the pandemic could do to families who lost loved ones, often the primary wage earner. I also saw how important our financial products are to the families who suffered the loss of a wage earner. In 2021, the increase in sales of life insurance policies was significant; in fact, it is the largest increase in a single year in the Order's history. While some may attribute the gains to good marketing or great salesmanship, there were other contributing factors that may have included families purchasing new or additional life insurance due to worries or concerns related to the pandemic and potential loss. This concern for protection of the family (assets) was Blessed Michael McGivney's primary aim in establishing the Order. I believe that the pandemic has brought us back to focus on the basic, or primary mission of the organization. Protection of the family and deepening of the faith of its members were paramount to Blessed Michael McGivney's dream of an organization that would truly play a significant role in the lives of Catholic families.

IMPACT ON CHARITABLE WORKS

Another significant area that has been impacted by the pandemic is that of our charitable works. Many of our normal programs that involved in-person activities and events had to be cancelled, resulting in a loss of donations. The charities that we support not only lost funds normally provided by the Knights of Columbus, but they suffered loss of donations from other sources as well. Local councils continued to solicit funds as best they could; however, a significant downturn in contributions was noted throughout 2020 and 2021. New virtual giving pages were developed and implemented on websites and social media; this helped bridge the gap between the traditional methods and new programs and opportunities that utilized virtual sites. While social distancing and masking guidelines allowed for some in-person events, these were still not as well attended or received as those prior to the imposed restrictions during the pandemic. Hopefully, in time, these newer methods of fundraising as well as being able to resume some traditional methods will result in increased donations and funding of the great charitable works that we promote.

CHAPTER 10

Members, Programs, Charity

I often wonder whether Blessed Michael McGivney envisioned the Order growing to over two million members? He made it clear that he believed we should have a presence in every parish, that protecting the family unit and deepening the faith of the men who would be Knights were of utmost importance and that in order to achieve these goals we would have to find a way to share this opportunity with every Catholic man who was over the age of 18 and in communion with the Church, that is to say, a "Practical Catholic."

To achieve our founder's dream and to continue to be

able to offer the many charitable programs, grants and services, we must continue to grow in our numbers as well as in our ability to attract the kind of men who want to be a part of something greater than themselves. As we become larger, the challenge to constantly grow becomes more and more difficult to achieve. This is due in part to the fact that every year we lose a percentage of our membership to death; another percent to age related non-participation and/or disability; still, another percent to people who leave the Church or just no longer want to participate. So, every year we must work to replace those lost members before we can count any gains in our overall number.

E-MEMBERSHIP

The Order has made significant strides in reducing barriers to entry in recent years. But more must be done if we are to continue to be a relevant factor in Catholic life. I believe the addition of the E-Member category was a significant step in the right direction. It takes into consideration the new "modern family," that is, family life in which both husband and wife may work outside the home and share in the child-raising duties, each being fully involved and committed. This new modern family often has life scheduled down to the minute with little unscripted time and in many cases, the free time or unscripted time is spent together. So, this new family structure may not include much time for the man to spend alone or away from the family. Councils must take this into consideration and consider more programs and events that allow for the full family to become involved. Programs and events that are inclusive will attract new members and have supportive families. Still, there are many younger members who just don't have the time right now to get involved with programs, activities, or council projects. For these men who want to be associated with what we stand for, and to be able to access our insurance and financial products, the E-Member program was a great alternative.

The E-Member program really was a significant factor in keeping the Order moving forward during the Pandemic of 2020. It made it possible to use electronic means to register for membership, be approved and receive a membership number. The E-Member program bypassed the need for local councils to have to conduct in-person degree ceremonials in order to get a new member into the Order.

By Summer of 2020, virtually all Catholic churches in the Americas had closed their doors to the public and were transitioning to offering Mass via live-stream. The Order had, prior to the 2020 pandemic, begun the transition to the new combined degree of Charity, Unity and Fraternity, which was, for the first time, open to family members to observe. By removing the need for secrecy, under the open format it was now possible to offer the ceremonials (degrees) via live-streaming. The Supreme Council produced a video of the new combined degree and broadcast this on several occasions; it was so popular that they began to offer the degree more frequently.

In Florida, we took the initiative to form regional teams and stream a Live Degree every Thursday. By offering the live degree on a regular basis, we gave local councils a means of bringing candidates into the Order as Third Degree members without them having to physically attend an event. The live virtual degrees continue to this day and contribute to the growth of the Order. The E-Member program was and is a simple means of providing Catholic men, over the age of 18 and practicing their faith as "Practical" Catholics, a simple way to join the organization and to access our insurance products.

FINANCIAL PROTECTION

One of the significant factors of the pandemic was the increase in demand for life insurance. I do not think I know any person who was not affected by the COVID-19 Pandemic. Everyone I know either contracted a version of this virus, had a friend or family member contract it, or, in many cases knew someone who died as a result of it. The Pandemic changed people's attitudes towards insurance. In many cases, people were reminded of their own mortality and how the virus can affect anyone, not just the old and infirm. We were all reminded, during the time in which churches were closed and Mass was only available to view on live-streaming, how important our Faith is to us; how when we are separated from the Eucharist, we feel sad and we long for the day when we can again share in the real presence of Jesus Christ through Holy Communion.

Being invited to operate the camera for live-streaming of Mass, during the pandemic, and to be invited to dine with Monsignor Tom on Sundays during the lockdown; this, was truly a Godsend. I had only recently been widowed and was living alone, so being invited to participate in the Mass, receive Communion and share in Sunday dinner was the highlight of my week during the time of the Church closures.

PROGRAMS OF CHARITY

One of the charitable giving programs that I wanted to make sure would continue during the pandemic, was the fundraising that we did to support vocations programs and, more specifically, the seminarians in our two Florida seminaries. During the pandemic, the students were sequestered in the seminaries and were not allowed to leave the campus. They normally would be free to visit friends and family on weekends and holidays, but now they were being kept secluded. Many were not able to get professional haircuts, make appointments or take care of things that were usually possible before the pandemic.

Being able to continue our support became a challenge. We had to come up with virtual events that continued awareness of their needs as well as ideas that could be continued at the council levels without having to make physical contact. One of the programs to support seminarians was the initiation of the "Ride for Vocations," now an annual event in which motorcycle riders can pay an entry fee (proceeds go to the fund) which gives them a patch, some other branded items and a dinner ticket. The riders start out with Mass in honor of Vocations Support, celebrated by the bishop of the local diocese; in this case the Archbishop of Miami, then they ride up through the middle of the state, stopping along the way to pick up additional donations from local councils. The ride ends outside of our state convention location and is concluded with a barbecue dinner and some other fundraising. Social distancing and masks were worn by the participants at the very first event, but that did not keep spirits down.

Robert "Bob" Anderson passed away in January 2022, having been a member of the Knights of Columbus for over 64 years; he had served as State Deputy and Vice Supreme Master of the DeSoto Province.

One of the things that I believe made a significant difference in membership recruitment during the pandemic was the fact that people really are social creatures, I think people forgot how much they miss being with other people in social events. Establishing charitable programs and events that draw people out to help provide a means for us to feel good about our activities. When these opportunities are well thought out and conducted safely with proper protocol in place, then it shows the true goodness of our organization, and that is an attraction to men looking for something to belong to that helps to define who they are.

CHAPTER 11

Overcoming the Odds

K nights of Columbus Fraternal Operations rely heavily upon the subordinate councils, including state and local levels to do the bulk of membership recruitment. Recruitment of new members is the lifeblood of any non-profit organization that wants to sustain its operations indefinitely. At the time when the COVID-19 Pandemic first impacted the United States of America, the Knights of Columbus had been operating continuously for nearly 140 years and, for the most part, had enjoyed steady growth. Florida is a Division One jurisdiction with one of the largest membership within the United States;

only a handful like California and Texas are larger. As a premier jurisdiction, the Order looks to Florida as well as the other Division One jurisdictions to carry the heavy load of recruiting new members. In fact, most new members coming into the Order are brought in through the handful of Division One's. The smaller divisions combined make up a minority of the intake of membership. The reason that I mention the significance of the work that the Division One jurisdictions perform is so that you can understand how much the entire Order depends on these large jurisdictions to effectively do their job and to reach their established goals for membership gain.

Several factors really played a significant role in the success that Florida experienced in membership gains during the pandemic. First, since we had instituted a monthly on-line meeting for all leadership of the state jurisdiction, starting on July 1, 2019, and continuing through June 30 of 2021, we had a jump on the training process. In particular, Grand Knights and District Deputies needed to have monthly contact with the various officers, directors, and committee chairmen who operate the programs and charitable events throughout the state. They needed to hear what was going on, to be able to share ideas and to understand that they were not alone, that the Knights of Columbus was going to continue to support local parishes; we were going to make this our finest hour.

Second, since the Supreme Council had recently introduced the new degree of Charity, Unity and Fraternity, which was open to all to observe, it effectively eliminated the need for "secrecy" regarding the ceremonials. We were able to transition this new combined degree into a virtual presentation that could be streamed live via the Internet, and we were having success with it. We already had been using a virtual meeting platform for our monthly leadership meetings and we were also planning on using it for broadcast of the three major events that take place each year, namely: State Convention; State Organizational Meeting; and the State Mid-Year Meeting. Having gotten used to logging in and participating in virtual meetings, our membership at the local council level was able to adjust fairly quickly to the new operations.

A third advantage that we had going for us was a fairly large number of former 3rd Degree teams including Conferring Officers, who were available in key areas of our state. These old degree teams were, in many cases, able to regroup, learn the new degree parts and be able to conduct the virtual live degree. The teams rotated so that each would have at least one degree per month. The virtual degrees performed by regional teams has been a platform that allows for a high degree of professionalism in the presentations and, as I previously mentioned, provided an opportunity for the State Deputy to speak directly to all new candidates at the end of the degree.

This fraternal greeting by the State Deputy was a personalized experience for each of the new members. A list of names of the new members was sent to the State Deputy, and prior to the end of the degree, he would read each name and congratulate each candidate and his family, separately, thus keeping the ceremonial on a personal level. I can say with certainty that this new ceremonial has had a very positive effect on the families of new members, especially the wives of new members who were present when their husband or son took the degree. Often, I would see wives sitting next to their candidate husbands and they would participate in the ceremony, placing the rosary on the clasped hands of their husband at the appropriate time in the ceremony. In each case, the State Deputy making a point to thank the families of new members for their participation, and to encourage them to continue to support their family member who was now a Knight, would have positive results.

Supportive family members make a significant positive difference in the level of involvement by new members. It is always a good idea to make sure the family is involved at an early date, and that the family is encouraged to continue to participate in activities of the local council, whenever possible.

The new combined degree of Charity, Unity and Fraternity also makes it possible for newer members to quickly advance to the 4th Degree. We know that historically, once a member becomes a 4th Degree Knight, he typically will be active for the remainder of his life. However, there is still no substitution for a live in-person experience, using both in-person degrees conducted with live-streaming as well as local in-person degrees; this will be a method that should result in the best possible experience for all potential candidates and members. Many people are not able to attend in-person events due to multiple reasons; for them, the option to attend the event virtually gives them the connection to other members that had been missing. For those who prefer and/or are able to attend the events in-person, their experiences are enhanced by the experience of being with a live community filled with other members.

As I think back on the accomplishments of the Florida Jurisdiction during the 2020–2021 Fraternal Year, when the pandemic was having a significant impact on how organizations would function, I am profoundly grateful for the help and assistance that I received by so many members of our Order, especially members of our State Board of Directors and those closest to me in the administration.

Our state convention in May 2021 was one of the early events that people were again able to attend in person. This event culminated in Governor Ron DeSantis giving the keynote address to an enthusiastic audience.

The governor spoke for more than forty minutes about how we (Floridians) would overcome all obstacles to see that our state would quickly be getting back to business. Having the Governor speak at our convention gave everyone in attendance a sense of how important our organization is to both the state of Florida and the world.

Florida Governor Ron DeSantis, Florida State Convention, 2021.

CHAPTER 12

Thoughts and Admonitions

As I think back on my journey as a Knight of Columbus and the evolution of my service as a fraternal leader, I am often amazed at how fast the time seemed to pass. I can still remember taking my first degree. I recall how the degree felt like a college fraternity initiation ceremony. I had been invited to join a fraternity during college; however, since my father had died shortly after I began my college education, and his having died without much life insurance, I had to work my way through school. Working two and sometimes three part-time jobs did not allow for any extracurricular activities.

Seeing my friends, however, who had been able to join a fraternity, and who would identify with that group for the rest of their lives, did have an impact on me. I did think about how I may have missed out on a significant life experience. So, when I was participating in my First Degree, I could not help but think that this was my opportunity to be part of a fraternity, bonding with men who share my common faith and beliefs about family, church, and community.

I was impressed with the physical ceremony as I saw how much energy and feeling the men presenting the degree put into their craft; I saw and felt how deeply committed to the mission of the Order they were and how much joy they seemed to get in witnessing the expressions and emotions on the faces of the new members. I will never forget this experience, even though our degree ceremonies have changed a lot over the years. The underlying message of protecting the family, increasing the faith of the members, and building up the Church still come through loud and clear. Each time I participate in an exemplification,

I am gratified by the lessons we teach; I know that we are doing important works that we hope and pray are pleasing to God and are helping to build up the Church on earth. I have been part of exemplar teams for the better part of two decades. Over this time, I have seen many changes to each of the degrees, some changes being subtle and others major overhauls.

Yet change is inevitable in order to maintain relevancy in an ever-changing society and world. Cultures change and evolve, and so the Knights of Columbus must continue to evolve in order to meet the needs of its current and future members while maintaining its core principles and values. I believe the Knights of Columbus has achieved this and will continue to be the "opportunity of a lifetime" for new and future members.

I often reflect on my journey through the state council in the key leadership positions. The offices, including State Warden; State Advocate; State Treasurer; State Secretary and State Deputy, required a commitment of two years each, for a total of ten years. When I looked at the number of estimated hours, it added up to more than 16,000 volunteer hours spent. I was often asked, "Why do you do this? Are you being paid or how can you spend so much time on things that don't pay?"

GRACE AND BLESSING

When thinking about it, I could only answer the question with one word, "grace." I did it for the grace that God gives us. Grace is an amazing gift! It is probably the only gift that we as human beings of faith can take with us when we leave this earthly life. It is something that once given will never be taken away and every time you commit an act of unselfish charity you have received this gift directly from God.

I have experienced many moments of pure joy, moments often following events that provided an opportunity to help people less fortunate, or people with physical or intellectual challenges. Usually, the people who need the most help are often the first to offer you a kind word or to show an expression of gratitude. Whenever I am present at a Special Olympics event and see the determination and drive of the athletes and witness their strength of will, I get validation that our participation is right and just, and that we are doing something good and something that matters.

When I visit a dedication ceremony for the placement of a new ultrasound machine at a women's clinic and hear the stories of pregnant women who come in for the free checkup, having contemplated abortion and then changing their mind after seeing the scan and hearing the heartbeat of their unborn child, and choosing to give life to that child, I am emboldened that our work matters and that we must continue to attract new members to join our cause.

My journey as State Deputy during the time of the great Pandemic of 2020 was nothing like what I had expected to encounter. We had to plan and execute the first-ever virtual conventions both at the State and Supreme levels; we had virtual meetings (pictured below) and virtual degrees that no one would ever have thought could be instituted in such a short time. But the members of our Order are resourceful, and through the workings of the Holy Spirit and by God's grace, we not only survived, we thrived.

Florida delegates paricipating in the
2020 Supreme (virtual) Convention.

For anyone contemplating a run for State Deputy, the best advice I can offer is to put yourself in God's hands, work together with your bishops and priests to form plans for your term, well in advance of your election to the high office of State Deputy. Then, when you are elected, be prepared for the unexpected and do not be surprised if you must rework your plan many times along the way. Being adaptable and willing to consider other people's opinions will be required to achieve successful outcomes, which you will need if you want to have success in reaching your jurisdiction's goals and objectives.

I truly value the time I spent in the various offices of State Warden, State Advocate, State Treasurer, State Secretary and State Deputy; but the true value was not so much about completing each position as it was the journey: it was enjoying the work and the experiences that come with each position. It was meeting the many people along the way who would change my life, touch my soul and help me become the man that I am today.

The true value is in the giving: The experience of the giving of your time, your talent and often your treasure to fulfill God's plan for you in this life, so that you may hope to enjoy even more in the next.

CHAPTER 13

Supreme Board of Directors

One of the things that amazes every State Deputy, upon completing his term of office, is the speed in which his transition from the busiest man in the jurisdiction to being just another member, happens in an instant. The transition from 11:59 p.m. June 30 to 12:00 Midnight July 1, signifies the transfer of great responsibility from one administration to another. Suddenly, the emails diminish to a trickle, the mailbox is no longer full on a daily basis and the phone calls drop dramatically, except for the few people who are uninformed as to the change in administrations. Then you happily take great satisfaction in telling them that there is a new State Deputy and that they need to contact him for the answers they seek. There are still minor duties that you as the "Immediate Past State Deputy" carry out; however, for the most part, the new administration moves ahead with its staff and agenda, and you are kind of left behind. It is at that moment in time that you start to take stock in how busy you had been. You think about all the programs and projects with which you were involved, and the good works that your team had accomplished; then you start to ask yourself—what is next?

When you have been functioning at a high level of involvement as the "how to" person, being responsible for coming up with plans and solutions for things related to the jurisdiction's business, it can be a little disconcerting at first, when you had been involved at a high level with many outside programs such as Special Olympics, American Wheelchair Mission, Ultrasound Initiative, working with groups such as Cross Catholic Outreach and Food for the Poor. Thoughts of "what can I do to continue contributing to these most worthy causes?" creep into your head.

Awarded as Top Conributor for the Special Olympics, 2021.

As I mentioned earlier, I was blessed with an administration full of talented people possessing many varied skills that covered a wide range of areas. Our administration was able to overcome many obstacles and adversities during the pandemic and was able to innovate new ways of conducting the business of the Order in our jurisdiction. Many of the ideas for conducting virtual live degrees were developed in the Florida jurisdiction and later promoted by the Supreme Council to be adopted by other jurisdictions. I believe that the Supreme

Knight and other members of the Supreme Board of Directors took notice of the works that were being implemented in the Florida Jurisdiction, and that went a long way in my being considered for a new position as a member of the Supreme Board of Directors.

At the 139th Annual Meeting of the Knights of Columbus, held virtually in August of 2021, the new State Deputy of Florida, Rob Urrutia, made the nomination for me to be elected to the Supreme Council's Board of Directors. I was elected to serve out the unexpired term of a former Supreme officer who had stepped down earlier in the year. I would be only the fifth Supreme Director elected from the Florida jurisdiction, a jurisdiction that had been operating for 117 years.

After joining the board, I was appointed to several committees, including the Audit Committee and the Eastern States Committee. The committees are essential to the operation of the organization and, as such, take a high priority in my schedule. Each director is assigned several jurisdictions to monitor and to be able to bring back to the Supreme Knight and other board members any relevant information as to activities within those jurisdictions. I was really impressed by the level of professionalism on display by our Supreme board members and especially with the Supreme officers and executive leadership.

To a man, everyone working for the Knights of Columbus out of our headquarters in New Haven, Connecticut, has several gifts or talents in common, which I strongly believe factor into our overall success. First, every person whom you meet conveys the same sentiment that puts God first. They are grateful to be able to work in an environment that not only allows this conviction but supports it.

Second, everyone is highly supportive of the concept of Family. You see it in the presence of their children and families attending Mass, you hear it in the discussions about all that they do to support the "Family Unit." Blessed Michael McGivney's dream truly is becoming a reality, and the leadership of the organization is seeing to it that this reality continues through the generations.

Finally, everyone involved truly believes that their work within the organization matters and that we are continuing to build on the foundation established by Blessed Michael McGivney, some 140 years ago. They believe that everyone can contribute to this process, and that does make a difference. Being on the Board has already provided me with many new opportunities to meet people from all over the world, people with new experiences and ideas ready and willing to share with others so that we can continue to offer our unique experience to every eligible Catholic family through membership in our Order.

Shortly after being elected to the Board of Directors, I had the opportunity to travel to Saltillo, Mexico, with the American Wheelchair Mission team. The Wheelchair Mission works through children's rehabilitation centers (known as *Centro de Rehabilitación Infantil Teletón* or CRIT). We were there to deliver sixty wheelchairs to a local CRIT center, where children with mobility issues are treated. This experience was an amazing opportunity to see "Faith in Action" across borders. The sixty wheelchairs were made possible from a donation by the Texas State Council of the Knights of Columbus. They also provided funding for a 'first of its kind' wheelchair refurbishment center, located on the grounds of the CRIT.

We happened to be there for the dedication, and I was asked to join the President of American Wheelchair Mission, Chris Lewis (pictured here speaking at the 2021 State Convention), for the dedication ceremony. During the wheelchair distribution, we physically picked up and placed the recipients into the chairs. The gratitude and joy at receiving the gift of mobility is amazing to witness firsthand.

So many of the families of recipients were moved to tears, seeing that not only would their loved one be able to be more independent, but that it would also free up the caregivers to do other things.

I was able to give a report at the next Board of Directors meeting on the great effect that the program is having. While I was participating in the wheelchair placement, I was interviewed by the media staff of American Wheelchair Mission. This interview later was used in a promotional video for the mission, validating my theory that when you witness firsthand the act of charity and you share your thoughts, as I was able to do on the video, you provide others with an opportunity to share in your joy and to share in the grace that was given. This can then lead the others to also become involved in similar works of charity.

I later was able to visit the Archdiocese of Nassau, Bahamas, with State Chaplain Emeritus Monsignor Thomas Skindeleski. We had planned to visit with Most Reverend Patrick C. Pinder, Archbishop of Nassau, prior to the pandemic, but had to postpone the trip. We were going to discuss the possibility of bringing a volunteer work team of Knights to help with repairs and rebuilding efforts from hurricane Dorian. So, in March of 2022, we were finally able to make the trip and discuss with the archbishop his plans for rebuilding. Needs continue, no matter what. Finding resources and putting people together to do God's work will always be part of the mission. (See Epilogue.)

I am thankful for being able to be part of the Supreme Board of Directors, and for being able to continue to meet new and interesting people from all over the world. Most recently, with the situation in Ukraine, I am amazed at how well we Knights of Columbus were able to mobilize and put into action a plan to support the people who have been displaced by the war. Truly we are making a difference and building on the foundation established by our founder, Blessed Michael McGivney.

CHAPTER 14

Talking Points, Take-Away

As I think back on my journey as a Knight and what it has done for me, I recall the early days when I had first joined. I joined because I felt blessed. I had everything in my life going the way I wanted it to be going. My wife and children were all healthy and doing well in school and work, I was successful in business and had a nice home life; but there was something missing. It was joining the Knights of Columbus that first gave me the opportunity to "give something back." I remember serving breakfast at the parish after Sunday Mass; this was giving of my time and talent. I found out that I was pretty good at flipping pancakes and now felt a sense of belonging that I really had not had with work or other professional organizations. As I continued to advance through the chair offices and to bigger jobs and responsibilities, I would meet new people who shared my values and ideas about faith, family, and community. This involvement allowed me not only to expand my community of friends but also would prove to be invaluable in later years when I would be the one needing support. I mentioned earlier that my mother had moved to Florida to retire and to help me in my business. She also became very involved in helping out at my local council events; and when I became a District Deputy, she would attend the other councils' events that were in my district. Everyone knew my mother and looked forward to seeing this spunky eighty-year-old setting up tables for dinners and then helping to clean up afterwards. My mother sadly was stricken with Alzheimer's disease and, in 2010, she went to be with God. This was one of those times when I really needed the support of my brother Knights. They really did come to my assistance, from moving furniture to help with the funeral and services. I remember thinking to myself how grateful I was to have such a caring and supportive group around me.

Later, after my wife passed, I would see support from across the jurisdiction pour in. I never had the experience of being totally alone; there was always someone to talk with, either by phone or via internet and I was truly grateful for the comfort that comes with being part of a great network of caring individuals. I have already mentioned that within two years since my wife's passing, I attended twenty funerals. Each time I attend a funeral, it brings back thoughts of the family members that I have lost. In most cases, I am able to offer some words for the bereaved that indicate that God's plan is one we cannot possibly understand as humans; but knowing that He loves us and wants us to be happy, offers the possibility that through faith, there is hope. The kind of hope that brings a sense of being able to be happy again. This does not mean that the loss will ever be forgotten, but that, in time, comes acceptance, and with acceptance comes the understanding that we must live our lives each day, enjoy every day to the fullest and be open to being happy. For me, being present during charitable events, helping those less fortunate and being able to continue to serve the needs of others, building up the Church, is a gift. It not only gives me a sense of purpose and belonging, but it validates my faith, and the return is that I receive grace from God. Grace is a gift that you get to keep, now and forever. It is one of the things that you do get to take with you on your journey after this life. So, no matter what life throws at you, if you maintain your faith in God's plan for you and you recognize that it is not about what you want, but what He wants for you. Then, you will be well on your way to a happy and productive life. For me service in the Knights of Columbus was my way to "Give Back." For you, your path may be different: but no matter what path you take, put all your talent and effort into it so that at the end of your life's journey you will be welcomed into heaven with the words "Well done, my good and faithful servant."

CHAPTER 15

The Future and Beyond

No individual can predict with certainty what the future will be like. We make predictions based on past experiences, historical records, trends, weather, seasons, and other cyclic events, but all of these are, at best, predictions. As an example, if you are planning an outdoor event several months in advance, let us say June 25, you may look at the weather reports for that specific time of the year. If it is during a time when rain is frequent, you may want to include having a tent or securing other shelter, to insure against rainout. Statistical analysis can help with the prediction, reviewing many years of weather reports for the June 25th date range over time. Then determining what you believe is a good sample size, such as the past 100 years, would give you a good idea. Counting the number of times there was rain on June 25th and then counting the number of times there was no rain will give you the remaining data needed to complete your analysis. If the ratio of rain days to dry days is close, in other words, 50/50, then it would be prudent to assume that your event is just as likely to get wet as it is to be dry. If, on the other hand, the data showed that the number of times it rained on June 25th was much less or more, then you would have a better understanding of what you need to plan for. Significantly more dry days may mean that you go ahead with your plan, but have a contingency for rain. Significantly more rain days may mean that you select an alternate date where there is less chance for rain, or you plan to have proper rain protection in place. Going back to the example, our survey took into consideration the period covering 100 years, or a century of time. By human standards, 100 years is more than the average lifetime, so most people will not see more than what occurs in this period. However, if we look at it from a 1,000-year period, 100 years is not very much. If we had been able to increase our study of the weather on our given date over a 1,000-year period, could we have gotten a much better survey of times it rained or did not rain on that date? Perhaps, or perhaps not; the 100-year study probably gave us a fairly accurate look; the longer survey may not be necessary for our determination. Predictability is the key, but still there is no guarantee that conditions could change on any given year, which may alter the outcome.

- "The best way to predict the future is to create it." — Abraham Lincoln
- "The future starts today, not tomorrow." — St. John Paul II
- "The work we do today is based on what we learned in the past, in order to have hope for our future." — Scott O'Connor

Looking back at my time as a State Deputy during the COVID-19 Pandemic of 2020, I am proud of the accomplishments that we achieved, and they were many; but there are things that we still could have done better, faster, and more efficiently. A pilot trains for every possible contingency that can be thought of, but things still occur that are outside the training. In those instances, they have to rely not only upon the training, but upon their skills, and finally their belief or confidence in themselves.

- "We need to try to do the right thing every time, to perform at our best, because we never know which moment in our lives we'll be judged on." — Captain Chesley B (Sully) Sullenberger
- "Tomorrow hopes we have learned something from yesterday." — John Wayne
- "However difficult life may seem, there is always something you can do and succeed at." — Stephen Hawking

The point that I am trying to convey is that it is our duty and our obligation, as current leaders of our organization to always be mindful of how well we are preparing for the future. Since we cannot predict with any certainty, significant directional shifts in the world, such as the date a war may break out, the date of the next major earthquake, fire, tsunami, or other disaster or when the next 100-year pandemic may affect us, we must train for every possible contingency that we can think of, and then trust in our training and our own abilities. Finally, we must always trust in God, for it is God's plan that we are all a part of, all destined to participate in, and if we have planned and paid attention to the details, a plan that we can follow God's lead to achieve. With the Holy Spirit as our Navigator, who can be against us? We will continue to build upon the dream of Blessed Michael McGivney, to strive to offer the benefits of membership in our Order to every eligible Catholic man and his family and to build up His Church.

For me, the work I am doing today is very fulfilling, I stay busy with my consulting business and local council and assembly participation. I can continue to contribute to the good of the Order, and hopefully, help with shaping the future. I also mentioned earlier that we must be open to being happy, that life offers each of us a new chance, every day, to make a difference. I have made many friends through my connections with the Knights of Columbus, I value each and every one of them. For me, the rewards are in the giving. I always get so much more in terms of joy and happiness from service than from anything else I can conceive.

Finally, I hope that anyone who reads this book can take away from my shared experience the knowledge that whenever you face difficult times, even when you think the world is crashing in on you, that we must keep our faith, that God does have a plan for us and that no matter what, He will not abandon you; neither will the Knights of Columbus.

EPILOGUE

Marsh Harbour

In August of 2022, in keeping the promise I made to Most Reverend Patrick Pinder, Archbishop of Nassau, Bahamas, to provide a team of Florida Knights to help with the rebuilding efforts, we were able to bring nine Knights, including State Chaplain Emeritus Monsignor Thomas Skindeleski, Past State Deputy and former District Master (Florida) Robert Read, current Florida District Master John O'Toole and several members of the St. Vincent Ferrer Council No. 13996, Delray Beach, to the island of Abaco.

The team (as pictured opposite) spent eight days working on the St. Francis de Sales Catholic School, building two playgrounds, a full scale basketball court, completing painting and landscape work in order to prepare for the school year. The team accomplished much in the week they spent, Monsignor Tom celebrated Mass every day in the Administration building with Archbishop Pinder joining us in the middle of the week. The Archbishop celebrated Mass with the team in the new school administration building kitchen, as depicted here.

L to R: Most Reverend Patrick C. Pinder, Archbishop of Nassau; Monsignor Thomas Skindeleski concelebrating Mass.

On Sunday, prior to departing for the journey back to Florida, Msgr. Skindeleski celebrated Mass at the St. Francis de Sales Catholic Church, located across the street from the school. It was the first Mass celebrated by a priest in over a year. Typically, the church has a deacon fly in from Nassau on Sundays, to conduct a Holy Communion service. It was a special treat for our team to be able to provide this service for the locals.

Florida Knights of Columbus rebuilding team, St. Francis de Sales
Catholic School, Commonwealth of The Bahamas, August 2022.

Inside rear cover: (Upper) Scott O'Connor with the American Wheelchair Mission, Saltillo, Mexico, October 2021.
(Lower) Knights of Columbus Color Corps, St. Katharine Drexel Catholic
Church, Weston, Fla., Spring 2007. L to R foreground: In green accent
is Tommy Thompson; purple, John O'Toole, white, Scott O'Connor;
purple, Pat Fittipaldi; white, Robert Dytkowski.

CPSIA information can be obtained
at www.ICGtesting.com
Printed in the USA
JSHW030944080123
35825JS00001B/26